Retired at 48

One Couple's Journey to a Pensionless Retirement

Retired at 48

One Couple's Journey to a Pensionless Retirement

A.R. English

Published by Iguana Books
720 Bathurst Street, Suite 303
Toronto, Ontario, Canada
M5S 2R4

Publisher: Greg Ioannou
Editor: Andrea Douglas
Front cover design: Jane Awde Goodwin
Book layout and design: Stephanie Martin

English, A. R., 1963-
Retired at 48 : one couple's journey to pensionless retirement / A.R. English ; editor, Andrea Douglas.

Issued also in electronic formats.
ISBN 978-1-927403-45-75

1. Retirement income--Canada--Planning. 2. Finance, Personal--Canada. 3. English, A. R., 1963-. I. Title. II. Title: Retired at forty-eight.

HG179.E54 2013 332.024'0140971 C2012-908583-9

This is an original print edition of *Retired at 48: One Couple's Journey to a Pensionless Retirement.*

Table of Contents

List of Figures

Introduction

We are a middle-aged married couple living in Toronto, without children, in a mortgage-free home. We each had successful professional careers, but it had always been our goal to retire early. By retirement, we mean no longer having to work anymore, ever. We do not mean trading in an initial career to take on a less-demanding or less-stressful job, probably for less pay. Work never defined us and was merely a way to make money so that we could enjoy life. There was so much that we wanted to do, but there was never enough time on the weekends or on our all-too-brief vacation days. So the sooner we could dispense with work and get on with life, the better.

Unfortunately, neither of us was forward-thinking or wise enough to pick a career that would provide us with an actual pension — that blessed concept where once you retire, your employer would continue to pay you a regular sum of money for the rest of your life. We each had a locked-in defined contribution RRSP to which our company would contribute only while we were still working. So our retirements would have to be funded from these meagre and insufficient sums, along with whatever we could save on our own. The money we accumulated when we walked away from our jobs would have to last us for the rest of our lives.

This was a daunting prospect, fraught with risks and dangers. How would we know whether we would have enough money to last our lifetimes? How long would we live? How would inflation affect us? What would the markets do? Much thought, research and careful planning would have to go into our retirement preparations.

We are by no means financial experts trying to offer advice or provide the magic answer. We didn't win the lottery. We didn't inherit a pile of money. We didn't invest in Apple or Google at rock-bottom prices and make a killing. Rather, we are just two reasonably intelligent, extremely motivated people who had a common goal and worked hard to achieve it.

We have been asked by so many people how we were able to achieve early retirement that we thought it would be best to write about our experiences. Our specific personal circumstances and situation probably won't apply exactly to everyone else. But some of the general concepts that we followed, our thought processes, and the practical descriptions and examples of what we did and how we did it just might be useful. Regardless of whether early retirement is in the cards or not, anyone without a pension needs to consider what amount of savings is required to retire on and whether that amount will last his or her expected lifetime.

The following recounts our path to achieving early retirement without a pension at age 48.

Dedication

This book is dedicated to Jean Allen English, an extraordinary woman who was ahead of her time.

Born in 1887, Jean Allen was the eldest of eight children living on a farm in Comber, Ontario. At the age of 14, she overheard her parents describe her as "the homely one that would probably never marry and therefore would stay on the farm to take care of them." As an intelligent, determined and self-sufficient adolescent, Jean was not prepared to accept this fate planned for her. Shortly after, she left home, got herself trained as a telegraph operator, and moved from job to job across Ontario. Jean was very skilled in her work and gained the reputation as one of the top telegraphers of either gender.

In 1915, Jean moved to the Patterson Grain Company on the Winnipeg Grain Exchange. While there, she began trading stocks for the company and once cornered the market in barley. Using the investment experience gained on the job, Jean made wise personal trades as well. By 1920, she was the highest paid woman on the grain exchange, owned several houses, and drove a Model T Ford. This was a rare and impressive accomplishment for a woman to achieve in that era.

Overworked and requiring a vacation, Jean decided to buy a remote 4-acre island on Lake Minnitaki, Ontario, as a vacation property. She commissioned a log cabin to be built on it and travelled by boat from Sioux Lookout, Ontario, to reach it each summer. One day while Jean was at the island, she had a visitor. Homer English, a superintendent with the Canadian National Railway was in the area to inspect railway districts. Upon hearing of this unusual woman who owned an island in the wilderness, Homer wanted to check it out. Romance bloomed, the two were married in 1925, and they had one child together.

Jean retired after marriage, as women were expected to do in those days, but she continued on with her wise investments and did quite well. After Homer retired, their family lived largely on these investments and used them to put their son through university.

Grandma Jean has been an inspiration to us, and by her example, showed us the value of financial independence. "English Island" is still in the family, and four generations have continued to make regular treks to vacation there. Now that we are retired, we will have even more time to spend up there, enjoying her legacy.

What Type of Retirement Do We Want?

Before we could calculate how much money we would need to support our retirement, we had to determine what we wanted our retirement to be like. We knew we didn't want to have to stay home and eat Kraft Dinner every night, but we had to be realistic and pick a scenario that would make us happy and still be achievable.

We realized that if we wanted to live a jet-setting lifestyle even though we had not had the foresight to be born into a family with the last names of Gates, Buffett or Jolie-Pitt, then early retirement was probably not in the cards. On the other hand, there were articles indicating that if we were willing to move to the Philippines, we could live quite well on $800 per month, and we could probably have retired years ago. Our plans were somewhere in between these two extremes.

We considered whether we wanted to live in another city, or another home. We had friends who planned to downsize from their large homes to smaller accommodations, or move to a smaller town with a slower pace, or live full-time at their summer cottages, or even relocate to Europe for a total change of lifestyle. Luckily we already owned our perfect, mortgage-free condo in a city and location that we loved, and could not imagine living anywhere else. We needed to make no changes in this respect. Unfortunately, this also meant that we would not be able to count on any cost savings or influx of capital that would result from downsizing our accommodations.

In determining what type of lifestyle we wanted after retirement, we considered all the activities we enjoyed and wanted to do more of, as well as all the new interests that we've always wanted to try but never had enough time to pursue. We took an inventory of this wish list, quantified how often we would like to do each activity, and estimated how much it would cost. Any expenses above and beyond what we were spending in the working years would eventually be added to our "retirement budget."

We don't really have an extravagant lifestyle. Material things like fancy sports cars, designer clothes, expensive jewellery or art are not important to us. We don't have any super-expensive hobbies, and could be very happy spending time on activities that cost little or no money, such as reading or walking. Our major entertainment expenses go toward travel, dining out and live theatre. In making our budget, we did not want to have to compromise or skimp on any of these activities.

We wanted to make sure we could actually afford to enjoy our retirement. There was no point having all this extra free time if we did not have enough money to do some of the extra things we wanted. So how much would we need?

How Much Is Enough?

The most difficult part of retiring without a pension was being confident that we had saved enough to last our lifetimes. We both come from families whose members live to ripe old ages, so who knows how long that might be for us? Just for fun, we found this life expectancy calculator at media.nmfn.com/tnetwork/lifespan that told us we would live until age 97! A more comprehensive life expectancy calculator can be found at www.livingto100.com, but the site asked for an email address to contact us before providing the results, which was not what we were looking for.

Retiring early without a pension makes the problem incrementally worse. Each extra year that we no longer bring in income or expand our savings base significantly increases the total amount needed to last through our retirement. This has a double impact, since it means one less year for the investment base to compound in growth, and one more year of withdrawing from that base.

As an example, we took an arbitrary scenario and kept all factors constant except for the age of retirement to evaluate the impact. In our scenario, the current age was 40, the age of retirement was 65, and we planned to live until age 90. We played with the numbers in a retirement calculator (described later) until we got to a state where the investment total we had at age 65 would last us exactly to age 90, with just enough to spare for the funeral services. We modified the age of retirement from 65 to 64 and found that we ran out of money at age 88. Retiring at 63 caused us to run out of money at age 85, and retiring at 60 meant we had only enough money to last us until age 79.

We learned that what you actually need to live on after retirement may or may not be as much as you think. The traditional rule of thumb is that you require about 70% of the gross income that you make during working years in order to spend in your retirement years (before tax). We realized that this formula did not apply to us since we were being taxed at a higher tax bracket in the working years yet were still saving over 50% of our net income. We could not know for sure what we needed to spend until we created a budget of our current expenditures and compared our expense estimates with actual values over time.

Figuring out how much is enough was a two-step process for us. We needed to determine the following:

1. On average, how much do we plan to spend per month or year?
2. Assuming a final savings amount before retirement, how long would our money last?

How Much Do We Plan to Spend?

Before estimating how much we would need in the future, it was important to understand how much we were currently spending, and on what. We started out by making a list of what categories of expenses we currently incurred, as well as any additional expenses that would arise as a result of retirement. For example, cell phones previously paid by our employers would now be our responsibility. We separated these expenses into mandatory versus discretionary so that we could come up with a low and a high estimate. For discretionary items, we listed what was the maximum we planned to spend, as well as the minimum we could spend if we had to cut back. In some cases, the minimum could be zero if we determined we could not afford the expenditure within our budget.

Mandatory versus Discretionary Expenses

We categorized mandatory expenses as those required for basic survival, including shelter, utilities and food. We also included any fees for hobbies or activities that would cost too much to start and stop intermittently. Since we were trying to establish a monthly total, we took any annual charges, such as car or home insurance, and produced an average cost per month.

For us, this list consisted of the following:

- Condo fees
- Property taxes
- Heating, electricity, water fees
- Cable, Internet, phone, cell phones
- Groceries
- Sundries
- Car insurance, licence
- Car maintenance
- Home maintenance
- Home insurance
- Health insurance
- Medical, dental, vision expenses
- Hobbies: gym membership, tennis membership

We considered discretionary expenses as those that we could reduce or eliminate in any given month, to cover unexpected shortfalls in income or unexpected expenses. Again, we took any annual expenses and produced a monthly average.

- Dining out
- Entertainment/hobbies
    - Theatre, movies, concerts, other events
    - Art galleries, museums or other club memberships
    - General interest lessons or courses
- Vacations/travel
- Clothing
- Gas, parking
- Transit
- Gifts
- Miscellaneous (buffer for additional, unavoidable expenses)
- Savings for big expenses (new car, new appliances, home renovations, etc.)

Tracking Estimates versus Actual Spending

We came up with an estimate of how much we needed to spend each month by itemizing and estimating our regular expenditures and then averaging out annual expenses. We included both mandatory expenses that could not be eliminated and discretionary expenses that we wanted to spend money on but could live without or could reduce periodically if the need arose.

Baseline Estimate on Spreadsheet

We plotted all these figures into a spreadsheet to provide us with an initial low (reduced or eliminated discretionary expenses) and high (included maximums desired for all discretionary expenses) estimate in current dollars for monthly income flow requirements from our retirement funds. Multiplying by 12 gave us an average annual net income that we needed to generate from our retirement funds, after taxes.

In the section "Gross versus Net Income," we describe how we used an online tax calculator to determine the gross income (including money to pay taxes) that we needed to generate, as well as some tax-reducing strategies that we employed to bring this number down.

Tracking and Projecting Expenses in Quicken

Once we had our baseline estimates, we could then start comparing against our actual spending and money flow, which we kept track of using the money management and personal finance tool Quicken.

We have a chequing account from which all of our bills are paid and cash is withdrawn for spending that cannot be covered with a credit card. We try to have as many bills as possible automatically deducted from this account or charged to our credit card. This means that rather than worrying about paying the bills at the appropriate time, we just need to make sure the account has sufficient funds. Condo fees, heating, property taxes, phone, cable, Internet, cell phones, gym fees and car and medical insurance all fit into this category. Our credit card bill is manually paid using funds from this chequing account, since the amount changes each month. During the working years, our salaries, which funded all the expenses, were also automatically deposited into the same account. In the retirement years, we will need to transfer money from our retirement funds to pay the bills. Since chequing accounts typically pay little to no interest, we try to keep only enough of a balance in our account to cover expenses. Any excess money is transferred to a higher-interest savings account or contributed as part of our annual investment savings (see the section "High-Interest Savings Accounts").

Using Quicken, we created regularly scheduled transactions to represent all the expenses that are automatically withdrawn from the chequing account, a "placeholder" transaction to represent an average estimate for our monthly credit card bill, and deposit transactions for our salary payments. We also created scheduled transactions for expenses that would be charged to our credit card on a regular basis, such as newspaper subscriptions. (See Figure 1.)

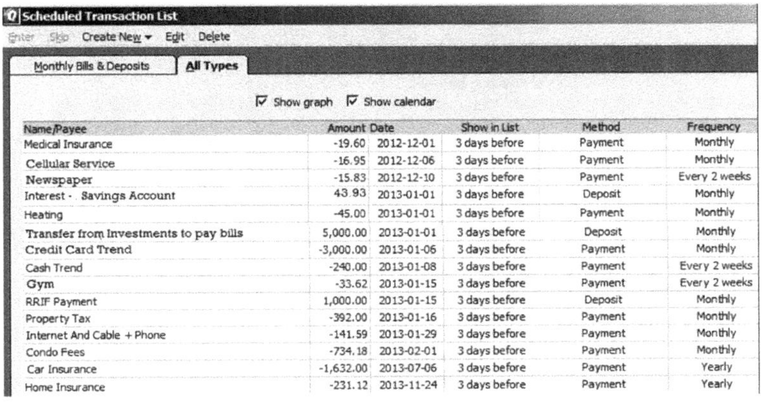

Scheduled Transaction List

Enter Skip Create New ▾ Edit Delete

Monthly Bills & Deposits | All Types

☑ Show graph ☑ Show calendar

Name/Payee	Amount	Date	Show in List	Method	Frequency
Medical Insurance	-19.60	2012-12-01	3 days before	Payment	Monthly
Cellular Service	-16.95	2012-12-06	3 days before	Payment	Monthly
Newspaper	-15.83	2012-12-10	3 days before	Payment	Every 2 weeks
Interest - Savings Account	43.93	2013-01-01	3 days before	Deposit	Monthly
Heating	-45.00	2013-01-01	3 days before	Payment	Monthly
Transfer from Investments to pay bills	5,000.00	2013-01-01	3 days before	Deposit	Monthly
Credit Card Trend	-3,000.00	2013-01-06	3 days before	Payment	Monthly
Cash Trend	-240.00	2013-01-08	3 days before	Payment	Every 2 weeks
Gym	-33.62	2013-01-15	3 days before	Payment	Every 2 weeks
RRIF Payment	1,000.00	2013-01-15	3 days before	Deposit	Monthly
Property Tax	-392.00	2013-01-16	3 days before	Payment	Monthly
Internet And Cable + Phone	-141.59	2013-01-29	3 days before	Payment	Monthly
Condo Fees	-734.18	2013-02-01	3 days before	Payment	Monthly
Car Insurance	-1,632.00	2013-07-06	3 days before	Payment	Yearly
Home Insurance	-231.12	2013-11-24	3 days before	Payment	Yearly

Figure 1: Quicken – Scheduled Transactions

We created a Quicken account that mirrored our bank chequing account and then applied the scheduled transactions to it for a month or more in advance. (See Figure 2.) This helped us forecast what our inflows and outflows would be, to ensure we always had enough money to cover our expenses. These predictions were reconciled regularly against the bank's online statements. Any one-time expenses or income would be manually added as an entry to this Quicken account. Setting up this forecasting tool during the working years prepared us for its use in the retirement years when it will become even more difficult to maintain proper cash flow for paying expenses. A side benefit is the ability to quickly and easily spot any fraudulent use of your bank account.

Quicken XG 2006 - QDATA - [PCF Chequing (C$)]
File Edit Tools Online Business Cash Flow Investing Property & Debt Planning Tax Reports Help
Back Update Reports Accounts Categories Yearly Cash Flow Monthly Spending Customize
PCF Chequing (C$) Register Overview
Delete Find Transfer Reconcile Write Cheques Set Up Online View Report Options How Do I?

Date	Num	Payee / Category	Memo	Payment / Exp	Clr	Deposit	Balance
2012-10-01		Transfer To Pay Bills / Bills Income	5230		c	5,000 00	6,128 48
2012-10-01		Condo Fees / Condo:Condo Fees		734 18	c		5,394 30
2012-10-01		Heating / Condo:Electricity		43 86	c		5,350 44
2012-10-05		Credit Card / Purchases	7414	3,420 76	c		2,384 18
2012-10-06		Gym membership / Entertainment:Gym		33 62	c		2,350 56
2012-10-16		Property Tax / Property Tax		392 00	c		1,958 56
2012-10-18		Hotdog / Dining		10 00	c		1,948 56
2012-10-23		Gym Membership / Entertainment:Gym		33 62	c		1,914 94
2012-10-24		Haircut / Clothing:Haircut		26 00	c		1,888 94
2012-10-24		Heat Vents / Condo:Home Repair		12 00	c		1,876 94
2012-10-25		Snacks / Dining		6 00	c		1,870 94
2012-10-28		Lunch / Dining		20 00	c		1,850 94
2012-10-29		Internet And Cable + Phone / Utilities:Cable TV		93 49	c		1,757 45
2012-11-01	DEP	Interest / Interest Inc			c	0 21	1,757 66

Figure 2: Quicken – Chequing Account with Projected Expenses for the Upcoming Month

Categorizing Expenses in Quicken

Next, we set up categories of expenses that we wanted to keep track of in order to determine how much we spent on our various mandatory and discretionary expenses. This would be used to compare our retirement budgetary estimates with actual expense figures year after year.

The major categories matched those within our estimates (e.g., entertainment), but for some categories, we also created sub-categories (e.g., tennis, theatre, movies) to get a more granular breakdown of expenses. (See Figure 3.) This would help us determine more discretely whether we should reduce or eliminate discretionary spending areas either temporarily or permanently in order to stay on budget.

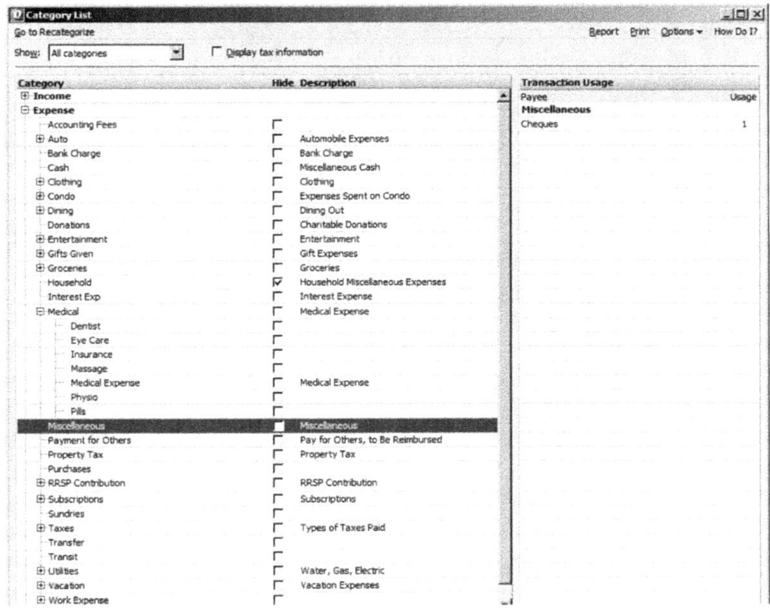

Figure 3: Quicken – Categories for Expenses and Income

Finally, we set up a Quicken account to represent our credit card purchases. (See Figure 4.) We entered each purchase manually so that we could properly categorize it to match our estimates. This may seem to be tedious or time-consuming, but it actually isn't if it is done regularly and incrementally. The Quicken credit card account is also reconciled on a periodic basis against the online credit card statement. The reconciliation process will pick up any purchases that were accidentally missed being added to Quicken. The regular cross-check provides the extra benefit of being able to verify that no fraudulent charges have been credited to your account.

There is an option in Quicken where you can automatically download transactions from the credit card account into the tool, thereby eliminating the manual entry. Other money management tools such as Microsoft Money support this as well. We chose not to use this feature. Though this could save time, we found that we do not have as much control over the categorizations of purchases or as much awareness of our spending habits and monthly totals. As our credit card balance grows, we update the transaction estimate in our Quicken chequing account to ensure that we will still have enough funds to pay the bill when it comes due.

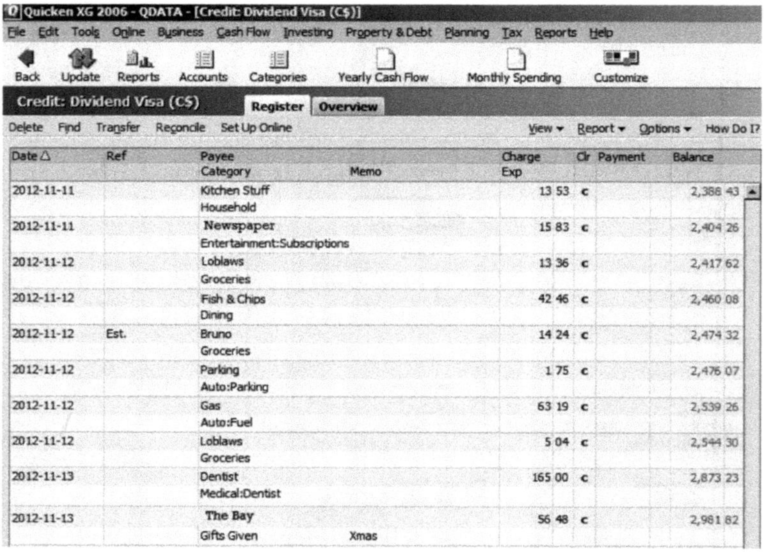

Quicken XG 2006 - QDATA - [Credit: Dividend Visa (C$)]

File Edit Tools Online Business Cash Flow Investing Property & Debt Planning Tax Reports Help

Back Update Reports Accounts Categories Yearly Cash Flow Monthly Spending Customize

Credit: Dividend Visa (C$) Register Overview

Delete Find Transfer Reconcile Set Up Online View Report Options How Do I?

Date	Ref	Payee / Category	Memo	Charge / Exp	Clr	Payment	Balance
2012-11-11		Kitchen Stuff / Household		13 53	c		2,388 43
2012-11-11		Newspaper / Entertainment:Subscriptions		15 83	c		2,404 26
2012-11-12		Loblaws / Groceries		13 36	c		2,417 62
2012-11-12		Fish & Chips / Dining		42 46	c		2,460 08
2012-11-12	Est.	Bruno / Groceries		14 24	c		2,474 32
2012-11-12		Parking / Auto:Parking		1 75	c		2,476 07
2012-11-12		Gas / Auto:Fuel		63 19	c		2,539 26
2012-11-12		Loblaws / Groceries		5 04	c		2,544 30
2012-11-13		Dentist / Medical:Dentist		165 00	c		2,873 23
2012-11-13		The Bay / Gifts Given	Xmas	56 48	c		2,981 82

Figure 4: Quicken – Credit Card Account

Reports in Quicken

The last step we implemented for tracking actual spending against estimates was to create reports in Quicken. Note that these reports are only as accurate as the data provided. Diligence in entering all expenses and properly categorizing them is rewarded with useful reports that reflect the reality of our spending habits.

We created a Yearly Inflow/Outflow Report that showed our inflows and outflows for each year. The report shows both the major and minor categories. (See Figure 5.) As each year passed, we developed a more accurate understanding of our expense needs, at least during the working years. We realized that some expenses would decrease and others would increase after retirement, and analyzed the projected impact of this. But at least this gave us a starting point for budgeting and estimating how much we would need in retirement years.

Yearly Inflow / Outflow Report

Date range: Custom dates Column: Year

2010-01-01 through 2012-12-31 (in Canadian Dollars)

Category Description	2010-01-01-2010-12-31	2011-01-01-2011-12-31	2012-01-01-2012-12-31
INFLOWS			
Bills Income	0.00	0.00	29,100.00
Other Inc			
PaymentReimbursement	681.43	806.00	798.00
Other Other Inc	0.00	389.44	20.00
TOTAL Other Inc	681.43	1,195.44	818.00
Parking Rental	1,215.00	1,400.00	0.00
Salary	76,722.96	99,448.46	38,528.42
TOTAL INFLOWS	**78,619.39**	**102,043.90**	**68,446.42**
OUTFLOWS			
Bank Charge	10.00	0.00	0.00
Cash	5,230.00	4,530.00	2,905.00
Clothing	1,635.29	1,456.48	1,014.73
Condo	14,644.59	17,614.07	13,351.82
Dining	3,532.99	6,156.75	5,078.06
Entertainment	6,475.23	5,186.36	11,249.12
Gifts Given	4,206.57	3,861.77	6,473.20
Groceries	6,421.33	6,800.32	7,133.74
Medical	868.60	1,203.38	2,138.84
Payment for Others	488.38	606.00	915.46
Property Tax	4,418.63	4,464.15	4,584.08
Sundries	1,122.02	904.86	630.07
Transit	726.00	1.010.00	679.50
Vacation	9,459.72	4,805.44	9,386.56
TOTAL OUTFLOWS	**59,239.35**	**58,599.58**	**65,540.18**
OVERALL TOTAL	**19,380.04**	**43,444.32**	**2,906.24**

Figure 5: Quicken – Yearly Inflow/Outflow Report

We also developed a Monthly Spending Report to understand how our expenses varied from month to month. (See Figure 6.) This was important because most of our bills had to be paid on a monthly basis, so we needed to be able to match monthly expenses with monthly revenue inflow. During the working years, this was easy since we both were paid on a monthly or bi-monthly basis. The trick was to generate an equivalent income flow during the retirement years.

We were able to see that some months would regularly be higher in expenses than others. For example, there were certain months when we tended to travel for vacation or dine out more often because the weather was nicer. There were spikes in months when a larger yearly expense, such as car insurance, came due. So we knew we had to structure our post-retirement income flow so that we always had enough to cover upcoming expenses. We also needed to be able to predict ahead of time what we would require for the next month. The groundwork we lay in setting up our tracking and prediction models in Quicken prepared us well for this.

A Review of Expenses

As we grew closer to reaching our retirement goals, we started to take a closer look at our expenses to see where they could be reduced.

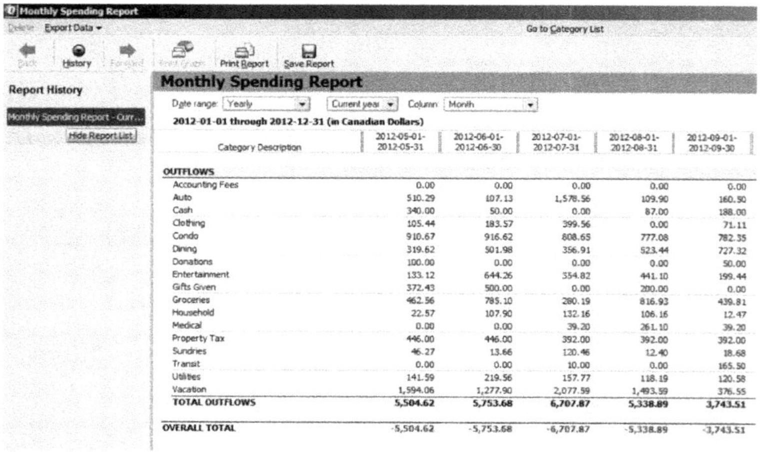

Monthly Spending Report

Export Data

History · Print Report · Save Report · Go to Category List

Report History

Monthly Spending Report - Curr...

Hide Report List

Monthly Spending Report

Date range: Yearly · Current year · Column: Month

2012-01-01 through 2012-12-31 (in Canadian Dollars)

Category Description	2012-05-01- 2012-05-31	2012-06-01- 2012-06-30	2012-07-01- 2012-07-31	2012-08-01- 2012-08-31	2012-09-01- 2012-09-30
OUTFLOWS					
Accounting Fees	0.00	0.00	0.00	0.00	0.00
Auto	510.29	107.13	1,578.56	109.90	160.50
Cash	340.00	50.00	0.00	87.00	188.00
Clothing	105.44	183.57	399.56	0.00	71.11
Condo	910.67	916.62	808.65	777.08	782.35
Dining	319.62	501.98	356.91	523.44	727.32
Donations	100.00	0.00	0.00	0.00	50.00
Entertainment	133.12	644.26	354.82	441.10	199.44
Gifts Given	372.43	500.00	0.00	200.00	0.00
Groceries	462.56	785.10	280.19	816.93	439.81
Household	22.57	107.90	132.16	106.16	12.47
Medical	0.00	0.00	39.20	261.10	39.20
Property Tax	446.00	446.00	392.00	392.00	392.00
Sundries	46.27	13.66	120.46	12.40	18.68
Transit	0.00	0.00	10.00	0.00	165.50
Utilities	141.59	219.56	157.77	118.19	120.58
Vacation	1,594.06	1,277.90	2,077.59	1,493.59	376.55
TOTAL OUTFLOWS	**5,504.62**	**5,753.68**	**6,707.87**	**5,338.89**	**3,743.51**
OVERALL TOTAL	-5,504.62	-5,753.68	-6,707.87	-5,338.89	-3,743.51

Figure 6: Quicken – Monthly Spending Report

Impact of Retirement on Expenses

We started by analyzing how retirement would affect the expenses that we incurred during the working years. There would be increases in some areas and decreases in others.

We determined that the following expenses would probably decrease or be eliminated after retirement:

- Expenses regarding travel to work: The cost of gas, car maintenance and insurance would all decline once the need to drive long distances to and from work on a daily basis was eliminated.
- Work clothes budget: Expenses related to dry-cleaning dress shirts and buying new clothes worn mainly for work would be drastically reduced.
- Work lunches: Regularly eating lunch at restaurants, or even at fast-food places, became a noticeable expense during the work years. Some of this would be replaced by higher grocery bills and pleasure lunches, but we expected the overall lunch expense to decline.
- Savings for retirement: A sizeable part of our joint incomes was being allocated to RRSPs, TFSAs and non-registered retirement savings. We would no longer be making new RRSP contributions after retirement, although we still planned to make TFSA contributions by moving money each year from our non-registered account.

Some expenses that would increase after retirement were ones that previously were being paid by our employers. These included the following:

- Cell phones and cell service fees
- Prescriptions for medicine
- Dental bills
- Health insurance
- Laptops or other portable computing devices

Other expenses that would increase after retirement were related to higher entertainment costs, since we had more time to play. The biggest and most costly increase would be in the area of travel. Groceries would probably increase as well, since we would be home more during the day and had the time to cook more-elaborate meals. This would to some degree offset the reduction of the cost of work lunches.

Where Expenses Might Be Reduced

The next step we took was to investigate areas where we could try to reduce expenses. The comparative information we list following was accurate at the time that we did our research. The specific information regarding rates, features or conditions offered by any company may no longer be relevant at the time of reading. Rather than taking anything in this section as a recommendation of what provider to go with for any given expense, it should be used instead to glean an understanding of the processes we followed as we searched for the best options in each case. All our analysis was done in today's dollar, with no consideration for inflation, since the inflation factor would be applied to our overall expenses when we calculated how long our money would last.

Cell Phone

Once we retired, for the first time we would have to be responsible for purchasing our own cell phones and paying for our own cell service. When examining cell phone costs, we evaluated our personal cell phone habits as opposed to how we used our company-paid cell phones while working. We acknowledged that we were not heavy cell phone users and hardly ever made personal cellular phone calls or sent text messages. What we did get used to with our work phones and wanted to keep was the ability to email and surf the Web. This drove the need for a smart phone but also influenced which cell service would best suit our particular needs. We were looking for a service that would provide us with the cheapest fees for low voice usage and high data usage. We also wanted to be able to use our cell phones on our travels without incurring exorbitant fees.

We used the following criteria as our base requirements for monthly usage for comparison purposes:

- 10 voice minutes, local calling
- 2 outgoing text messages (we never latched on to this texting craze)
- 0 voice minutes, long distance
- 500 MB data per month
- Voicemail required

Based on these requirements, we did a comparative analysis of various cell phone providers, taking into account the criteria that would impact us. This included the voice or talk rates, data rates for email or surfing, cell coverage areas, roaming charges or other rates for usage outside of Canada, types of phone supported, ease of buying more usage minutes (if applicable), and ease of bill payments. Since most companies offered multiple options based on usage volumes, we noted the one that best met our requirements. In doing this research, we reviewed each company's website, read their brochures and visited their outlets to further clarify the answers to our questions.

Here were the results that we found in second quarter, 2012. All estimated monthly costs excluded taxes and extra service charges. (See Figure 7.)

	Voice Plan						
Provider	Local	Canada /USA Long Distance	Text	Data Plan	Cost Calculation	Estimated Monthly Cost	Coverage Area
Bell	200 minutes, then $0.45 per minute	$0.45 / minute	Unlimited	100 MB $10 for extra 100 MB	$43 + $10/100 MB * 4	$83.00	Major populated areas across Canada
Rogers	$0.25 per minute $20 minimum	$0.45 / minute	Unlimited	100 MB $0.15/MB after	$20 + $0.15/MB*400	$80.00	Major populated areas across Canada
Telus	50 minutes	$0.45 / minute	$0.20 per text	Up to 500 MB is $30	$25 + $0.20/Text * 2 + $30 for 500 MB data	$55.40	Major populated areas across Canada
7-Eleven	$0.25 / minute $25 for 100 minutes - all top-ups last 365 days	$0.35 / minute	$0.10 per text	$10/month Unlimited data	$0.25/call * 10 + $0.10/text * 2 + $10 for data	**$12.70**	Major populated areas across Canada
Wind Mobile	$0.20 / minute Top-ups last 30-365 days $8 for voicemail	$0.20 / minute	$0.15 per text $0.25 international	$1/MB or $5/month + $0.20/MB after 50 MB	$0.20/call * 10 + $0.15/text * 2 + $0.20/MB * 450 + $5 data plan +	$105.30	Greater Toronto, Niagara Falls, Ottawa, London, Kitchener, Barrie, Kingston, Calgary, Edmonton, Vancouver and surrounding areas
Virgin	200 minutes	$0.45 / minute	Unlimited	1 GB	$63	$63.00	Most of the densely populated areas in Canada
Mobilicity	Unlimited	$0.20 / min USA $0.15 / min Canada	Unlimited	Unlimited	$45	$45.00	Vancouver, Calgary, Edmonton, Toronto, Ottawa and surrounding areas
Fido	Unlimited	$0.45 / minute	Unlimited	500 MB	$50	$50.00	Many densely populated areas in Canada No coverage in Saskatchewan

Figure 7: Cell Phone Comparisons

Based on our particular and possibly untraditional usage patterns, we decided that the best solution for us would be to go with the 7-Eleven SpeakOut service. They had the plan that provided the lowest data costs ($10/month for unlimited data), which made up the bulk of our usage, and an acceptable per-minute voice rate ($0.25 per minute), which would be insignificant in the monthly fees based on our low usage habits. An extra bonus was found in their top-up policies that allow us to buy cell minutes in the denominations of $25, $35, $50 and $100, which last for 365 days from the date of activation. Many of the other providers' top-up minutes expire anywhere between 30 to 90 days. SpeakOut also has a web interface that allows us to purchase extra minutes online, which is of great convenience.

In order to use the SpeakOut service, we needed to buy an unlocked smart phone, the Speakout SIM card, and a starting set of minutes plus the data plan. We were able to purchase an inexpensive, used older-model smart phone that met our needs. Having the unlocked phone provides an extra advantage for when we travel outside of Canada. We can simply buy a SIM card from the new country in order to have local cellular access without incurring massive roaming charges.

Our next dilemma was whether we needed one or two cell phones and whether they both needed to be smart phones with data plans. Again, we assessed our usage patterns and decided that the number of times when we would both be out separately and need to communicate with each other would be minimal. Our need did not justify the cost of a second smart phone with data. It did seem like a good idea to have a second phone for emergencies, if we could find an economical enough solution. Again, the SpeakOut plan offered the solution. Their lowest-end "dumb" phone cost only $39, and we could get a $20 discount if we bought $50 worth of minutes. We were able to use the $50 coupon against the smart phone and buy a $25 one to be used as a second phone that would barely be used at all. So we were able to get a $19 phone that will cost $25 a year to maintain.

The exercise of comparing all the different offerings from the various providers was educational and will be useful if we find our usage patterns change in the future. For now, this cell phone solution meets our requirements with very little capital outlay and low monthly fees.

Cable/Internet/Telephone

We had our cable, Internet and telephone service all coming from the same provider in order to receive a "bundle" discount.

We carefully reviewed each of these bills to determine whether we really needed the level of service that we were receiving. We decided based on our Internet usage habits that we did need the current speed and volume that was being provided. We considered cancelling our home phone and just relying on a cell phone, but were uncomfortable with this option. While we don't use our cell phones much, we do rely heavily on our home phone and find the reception and service within our dwelling to be more reliable. Since we had already found ways to minimize our cell phone bill based on low usage, we decided to continue to support both LAN line and cell service.

When we looked at our cable bill, we did find that we were not taking full advantage of the level of cable service that we were paying for. We were mainly watching the channels supported by basic cable and would not feel deprived by eliminating our high-definition service or hundreds of extra channels that we didn't watch. We were also starting to investigate watching movies or TV shows via Internet streaming to take advantage of the fact that we already paid for the Internet service. Reducing our cable service lowered our overall bill by 27%.

Then we took advantage of how competitive the major telecommunications companies were in terms of trying to win new customers or retain their existing base. When a rival provider offered up a great sale rate, we called up our current provider and told them we wanted to cancel and switch over. Immediately we were offered a matching rate as long as we agreed to stay with our provider for a minimum two-year period. Since we never really wanted the hassle of switching anyway, this was more than agreeable. The result was another 35% savings over our original rate when we first started this exercise.

So with a bit of due diligence, we reduced our telecommunication expenses by over 50%.

Health Insurance

Retiring early meant we would not receive any more company health benefits. The OHIP benefits for seniors (covering prescription drugs, dental services and home care) did not kick in until age 65. Thus, we were left on our own to pay for health insurance in order to cover medical, dental and vision bills not currently covered by OHIP. This led to an analysis of our current expenses and a comparison of various health insurance packages to determine which one might be the best fit at the lowest cost.

The following table shows a high and low estimate of our pre-retirement expenses that were covered by our companies' health insurance while we were working. We noted that the amounts were not that high and we could potentially pay for them ourselves. The concern was more about unexpected future ailments or issues that could lead to enormous fees that would not fit within our budget, and that could seriously deplete our retirement capital. We needed to review the terms of the insurance policies carefully to determine what protection we would have against this possibility.

Current Costs	High Estimate	Notes for High Estimate	Low Estimate	Notes for Low Estimate
Dentist – cleanings	$600	$300 cleanings × 2	$600	$300 cleanings × 2
Dentist – fillings, other preventative	$400	Fillings, etc.	$0	No extra work needed
Prescription drugs	$210	Current prescription	$210	Current prescription
Travel insurance	$195	30 days of travel	$65	14 days of travel
Eye checkups	$100	$100/2 years × 2	$50	$100/2 years × 2
Total	**$1505**		**$925**	

We looked at several major health insurance providers and evaluated their terms and rates. Using our current costs as a baseline, for each policy option, we calculated what the annual health care costs would be. We started with the premiums for the two of us, and then added on the extra fees that were not covered due to deductibles and maximums. (See Figure 8.)

As we suspected, by the time we factored in the premiums and the deductibles, for the most part, the costs significantly exceeded our current expenditures. And they all had maximums that limited the payout so that we would still be on the hook for large sums if we suddenly needed expensive medicines or other extraordinary care.

It became clear that we could self-insure for the regular expenses but needed some sort of catastrophic insurance to cover major unexpected events or critical illnesses. Our research came up with the following options: Unless we misunderstood the policy terms (which were really complicated in some cases), only Manulife seemed to provide payouts that spanned more than one year and did not limit the type of illness. Although the deductible was large, it was not insurmountable, and the premiums were low enough that we were not paying significantly for a situation that may never occur. Manulife was also the only choice that provided an easy-to-access online quote of the premiums. The others seemed to require direct contact with an agent, but since their coverage did not suit our needs, we didn't bother. None of the choices offered dental coverage, but it was unlikely that any dental bill would bankrupt us. We were more worried about cancer treatments or rare tropical diseases with treatment that could involve prohibitively expensive drugs or home care.

	Drugs	Dental	Vision	Travel					
Provider	% Coverage Yearly Maximums	% Coverage Yearly Maximums Preventative Frequency Restorative	% Coverage Yearly Maximum Frequency	% Covershr Life Maximum Length of Trip	Couple Health Insurance premiums - to age 54	Total Health Costs	Health Cost Formulas	Couple Health Insurance premiums: age 55-59	Couple Health Insurance premiums: age 60-64
Sun Life Basic	60% $750	60% $500 9 months None	NONE	NONE	$128/month $1536/year	$2,020	$1536 Fees + 0.4 x $210 drugs + 0.4 x $1000 dental + $0 for travel	$136/month $1632/year	$146/month $1752/year
Sun Life Standard	70% $100,000	70% $750 9 months None	100% $150/$50 exam 2 years	100% $1 million 60 days	$206/month $2472/year	$2,835	$2472 Fees + 0.3 x $210 drugs + 0.3 x $1000 dental + $0 for travel	$221/month $2652/year	$242/month $2904/year
Sun Life Enhanced	80% $100,000	80% $750 9 months 60% / $500 per year	100% $150/$50 exam 2 years	100% $1 million 60 days	$325/month $3900/year	$4,142	$3900 Fees + 0.2 x $210 drugs + 0.2 x $1000 dental + $0 for travel	$351/month $4212/year	$366/month $4392/year
Manulife Combo Starter	70% $525	70% 400 9 months None	100% $150/$50 exam 2 years	$5Million for 9 day trips	$71/month $852/year	$1,302	$852 Fees + 0.3 x $210 drugs + 0.3 x $1000 dental + $87 extra travel days		
Manulife Combo Basic	70%/90% $750/$4972	80% / 50% $300/$850 9 months None	100% $250/$50 exam 2 years	$5 million for 9 day trips	$84/month $1008/year	$1,568	$1008 Fees + 0.3 x $210 drugs + 0.2 x $300 dental + 0.5 x 700 dental + $87 extra travel days		
Manulife Combo Enhanced	90%/100% $2222/$8000	100%/60% $500/$700 9 months 60-80%/$400	100% $250/$50 exam 2 years	$5Million for 9 day trips	$141/month $1692/year	$2,000	$1692 fees + 0.1 x $210 drugs + 0.4 x 500 dental + $87 extra travel days		
Great-West Life Basic	100% $1200	85% $1000 9 months None	100% $200 incl exam 2 years	$1 million 30 days	$295/month $3540/year	$3,549	$3549 fees		

Figure 8: Health Insurance Comparisons

So our final decision was to forego regular insurance and purchase Manulife's Catastrophic Health Insurance. (See Figure 9.) Note that we needed to fill out an extensive medical form and pass a medical assessment to qualify.

		Drug	Home Care	Dental	
Provider	Age Limit	Deductible Coverage Max	Deductible Coverage Max		Mth/year Premiums for couple
Manulife Catastrophic	21–64	$4500 / year 100% after deductible Unlimited	$7500 / year 100% after deductible $25,000 / year - $100,000 lifetime	None	$32 $384
Sun Life Critical Illness Basic	18–50	none cancer, heart, stroke only one-time payout $50,000-$500,000		None	online quote unavailable
Sunlife Critical Illness	18–65	none 25+ illnesses one-time payout $25,000-$2.5 million for most illnesses		None	online quote unavailable
Great-West Life Critical Illness	25–65	none cancer, heart, stroke only one-time payout $10,000-$1 million (must last survival period)		None	online quote unavailable

Figure 9: Catastrophic/Critical Illness Insurance

When we were really responsible for our own yearly drug and dental expenses, we needed to examine options to minimize those costs.

Medical Expenses

During the work years when health benefits were covered by our employers, it was inconsequential for us to receive the "brand name" version of prescription drugs. Once we stopped working, we requested our pharmacies switch to the generic equivalent when available, since the price was significantly less than the brand name version. When we were removed from the restrictions placed upon drug renewals by our works' insurance companies, we could purchase drugs for six months at a time, as opposed to every three months, to save on the dispensing fee. We also shopped around for lower dispensing fees, comparing traditional pharmacies with those found in supermarkets and discount stores such as Costco.

Dental Bills

While we were covered by company insurance, we would be convinced by our dentists to come for more frequent checkups or cleaning, ranging from every four to six months. Once we were no longer covered, we negotiated with our dentists for a less aggressive schedule and settled on every nine months. We also informed them that we were not interested in discretionary, "nice to have" treatments such as extra fluoride, or teeth whitening, since we now had to pay for them ourselves. To our surprise, when we informed our dentist that we did not have company insurance and would be paying the bills ourselves, we were automatically charged a slightly lower rate.

Car Insurance

Not having to drive long distances to and from work every day significantly reduced our driving needs. Since we live in the heart of the city, we can walk or take transit to most places that we want to visit for fun during retirement. Therefore, a quick call to our auto insurance broker secured us an immediate reduction in our car insurance. We were also told to call back when we turn 65 or when we start collecting CPP for a further retirement discount. Unfortunately, this discount does not apply to early retirement.

Groceries and Sundries

When we were working, time was money and we could not always afford the time to look for the best price when buying groceries. Now that time was no longer a luxury, we could afford to shop around more and look for bargains or sales when it came to purchasing groceries and sundries. For example, we noticed that certain supermarkets discount their meats on Sundays, and our drugstore has regular promotional days when more items are on sale, or we can earn extra reward points.

We also had more time to enjoy the art of cooking, trying out new and more adventurous recipes. In addition to being enjoyable, this had the added benefit of reducing the overall cost of eating. In most cases, cooking at home would cost much less than dining out or even buying takeout. We could cook a hearty chicken dinner for two for around $10–$12, while a similar meal at even a modestly priced restaurant like Swiss Chalet would cost over $25.

Transportation

Once my employer stopped paying for my transit pass, the cost and value of transit as opposed to other means of transportation came into question. It is sad but true in our city that the full cost of a return trip for two people via public transit in many cases exceeds the cost of driving and parking (putting aside the implications on the environment for now). Therefore, we started to weigh our transportation options for each trip to decide on the most economical approach.

An even better option that is now afforded to us through the luxury of time is to walk. We now routinely walk up to 7 kilometres to get downtown and then take transit back home again, saving half the cost. It's better for the environment, and getting exercise, fresh air and good conversation are extra side benefits of this economically sound activity.

Entertainment

With a little bit of research, we were able to find many activities that we enjoy that either don't cost any money or offer discount opportunities. Most museums and art galleries have times when admissions are half price or free. Free festivals, concerts, historical and architectural walking tours, art walks and exhibitions are held throughout the city during various months of the year. In addition to lending books, our public libraries offer a variety of free activities. They hold author talks, book clubs and writers groups; run courses on a wide variety of topics; provide lessons on arts and crafts; show movies; and invite experts to give lectures on literary topics. In Toronto, there is a Museum and Arts pass that can be checked out from any library branch to gain free access to numerous arts and cultural venues. Perhaps other cities have something similar as well.

Travel

One of our largest anticipated increases in expenses after retirement was travel. We both love to travel and looked forward to the opportunity of taking more frequent and longer trips than we had time for during the working years. Thus it was extremely important to look for ways to minimize costs in this area, while not skimping on the locations or activities that we wanted to experience.

We tried to convince our friends and family that they should move to exotic locations so that we could stay with them, but this was not a very successful strategy. Luckily, there were more realistic options at our disposal once we were no longer restricted by time or requirements to plan vacation dates around work obligations.

If it is financially advantageous to us, we can travel mid week, take early morning or late-night flights, or travel at the last minute in order to pick up deals on airfare. Rather than taking multiple short trips, we can travel for longer durations on a single trip and have to pay the airfare only once. Many hotels and resorts offer weekly or monthly discounts for longer stays. We use travel websites such as Expedia (www.expedia.ca), Priceline (www.priceline.com) or Hotels.com (www.hotels.com) to search for cheaper flights, hotels or car rentals.

Using travel reward points such Air Canada's Aeroplan miles helps to bring down travel costs since you need to pay only for the taxes. Unfortunately there seem to be a disproportional amount of taxes related to airfare. Travelling farther afield not only costs more travel points but also seems to significantly increase the amount of taxes owed. We have found that it is more economical to use the travel points for closer trips and wait for seat sales for farther ones.

In order to save currency conversion costs every time we travel to the States, we have a US dollar non-registered account within our investment portfolio that contains a single US dividend-paying stock. We did not want to have too many US dividend stocks since they do not enjoy the same tax advantages as eligible Canadian dividend stocks. But we did want to have regular access to some US cash for when we travel in the United States. The US dividends from this stock can be transferred into a US chequing account that we opened for this purpose. Now we are able to withdraw US cash without incurring exchange rates or high service charges related to purchasing the currency from a bank or money exchange service.

The website Vacation Rentals by Owner (www.vrbo.com) cuts out the middleman and allows owners to offer their houses, apartments and condo suites directly to potential renters. As a result, the rates are usually even lower than for hotel rooms and the accommodations are much more spacious, including a kitchen and living area. Having a kitchen enables us to eat some meals at "home," which saves on the dining portion of our travel expenses.

One other way we planned to reduce travel costs was to continue to participate in home swaps. We had successfully completed two swaps in the past, once to Chicago and once to Paris. We signed up for a free home swap website called Geenee (www.geenee.com), which allows you to post information about your home and then contact other members to propose a swap. The home swap provides great savings on travel expenses since your accommodations are free. We have had no issues with our swaps, and in each case, returned to an immaculately clean home. For those who are worried about letting strangers stay in your home, you need to remember that you are also in theirs. We each treat the other's home as we would like ours to be treated. However, because Geenee is free, sometimes we find it hard to find swaps since some entries may have been added as a whim and do not represent serious swap opportunities. Now that we are retired, we plan to sign up for one or more paid websites, in hopes that by paying money to be on the site, the members are more serious about swapping.

A relatively new site called Love Home Swap (www.lovehomeswap.com) was offering a two-week trial for only $1 (with a subsequent annual fee of $159 per year), so we decided to try it out for the two weeks, and within that time period we entered into tentative negotiations for swapping with people from Italy, the Netherlands, Belgium and the United Kingdom. Given the much more promising results, we decided to continue on with the membership for a year to see how it goes.

If the Love Home Swap service does not result in successful swaps, we have our eye on several other sites, including HomeForExchange.com (www.homeforexchange.com), which costs $64 per year, Home Exchange (www.homeexchange.com), which costs $119.40 per year, and Intervac (www.intervac-homeexchange.com), which costs around $100 per year.

How Long Will the Money Last?

After we completed our analysis of the impact of retirement on our expenses, we revisited our expense budget spreadsheet and updated our budgetary estimates to reflect our findings. We made new budgetary estimates for what spending would look like after retirement, increasing or decreasing our expense categories where appropriate. Once we had a good grasp of how much we planned to spend on a year-to-year basis, we were in a position to calculate a target starting amount of retirement funds that we would have when we left our jobs.

Online Retirement Planner Tool

We found an excellent retirement planner that accepted our assumptions about various criteria and generated a report charting income growth during the working/savings years and then expenditures during the retirement years. Based on our inputs, it showed whether we would have enough money in our plans to meet our goals for our estimated duration of retirement, and if not, at what age we would run out of money.

The planner, from the *Globe and Mail*'s Globe Investor, can be found at the following address. (See also Figure 10.) You need a Java plug-in installed in your browser for the images to show up properly: www.globeinvestor.com/resources/personalfinance/rrsp/retirement_calc/CARetirementPlan.html

This calculator takes the following parameters as input:

- Ages
    - Current age
    - Age of retirement
    - Years of retirement
- Pre-retirement income
    - Current retirement savings (the starting point for the calculation)
    - Current gross annual income
    - Expected annual salary increase on average as a percentage
    - Pre-retirement rate of return from investments as a percentage
- Yearly savings for retirement, calculated as a percentage of gross annual income
- Rate of inflation as a percentage
- Post-retirement spending
    - Post-retirement rate of return as a percentage
    - Percent of retirement income (annual retirement spending as a percentage of final income)
    - Monthly company pension (if any — in our case, none)
    - Monthly Canada Pension Plan (CPP) or Quebec Pension Plan (QPP) (as a dollar amount)
    - Monthly Old Age Security (OAS) (as a dollar amount)

The tool applies the inflation percentage to the yearly calculations of annual retirement income and OAS/CPP payouts to reflect the increase in spending needs and increase in government pension allowances due to inflation.

Since my spouse and I treated our joint retirement savings as a single bucket, we combined our salaries, CPP and OAS amounts in the input parameters. Our ages were within one year of each other, so we picked the elder one.

After entering the parameters, pressing the “Calculate” button provides a summary graph showing whether you’ll have enough money to fund your estimated retirement years. This summary graph indicates either “You may need to save more” or “Your plan is on track.” Pressing the “View Report” button provides a detailed chart that shows the starting and ending balance for each year during your saving and spending years. If your plan will run out of money, the calculator shows at which year this will happen. (See Figure 11.)

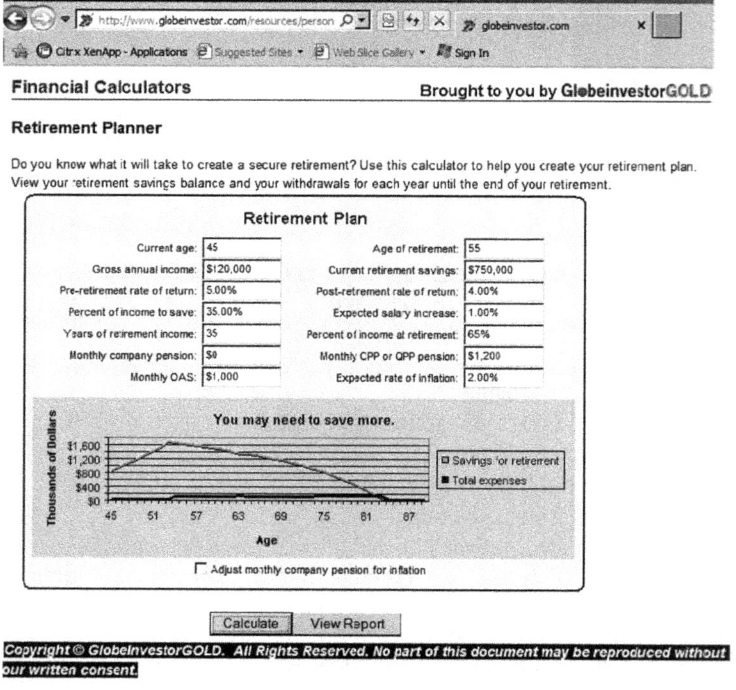

Figure 10: Retirement Planner Tool – Inputs and Summary View

By playing around with the input parameters, we tested out various scenarios that would allow us to make our plan. If we missed the target, we tried to adjust one of the following factors. Not all of these factors were realistically under our control, but it was still interesting to see what would happen:

- Age of retirement (how much longer we would have to work)
- Years of retirement (how long we would live)
- Percentage of income saved for retirement each year (how much money we were saving annually)
- Our salary or rate of salary increase (how much income we were bringing in)
- Expected rates of return either before or after retirement

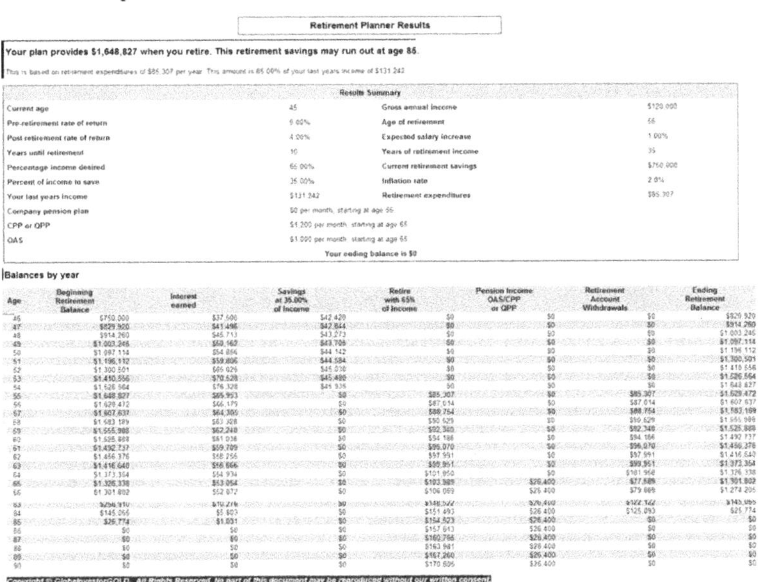

Retirement Planner Results

Your plan provides $1,648,827 when you retire. This retirement savings may run out at age 85.

This is based on retirement expenditures of $85,307 per year. This amount is 65.00% of your last years income of $131,242

Results Summary			
Current age	45	Gross annual income	$120,000
Pre-retirement rate of return	5.00%	Age of retirement	55
Post retirement rate of return	4.00%	Expected salary increase	1.00%
Years until retirement	10	Years of retirement income	35
Percentage income desired	65.00%	Current retirement savings	$750,000
Percent of income to save	35.00%	Inflation rate	2.0%
Your last years income	$131,242	Retirement expenditures	$85,307
Company pension plan	$0 per month, starting at age 55		
CPP or QPP	$1,200 per month, starting at age 65		
OAS	$1,000 per month, starting at age 65		
Your ending balance is $0			

Balances by year

Age	Beginning Retirement Balance	Interest earned	Savings at 35.00% of Income	Retire with 65% of Income	Pension Income OAS/CPP or QPP	Retirement Account Withdrawals	Ending Retirement Balance
46	$750,000	$37,500	$42,420	$0	$0	$0	$829,920
47	$829,920	$41,496	$42,844	$0	$0	$0	$914,260
48	$914,260	$45,713	$43,273	$0	$0	$0	$1,003,246
49	$1,003,246	$50,162	$43,706	$0	$0	$0	$1,097,114
50	$1,097,114	$54,856	$44,142	$0	$0	$0	$1,196,112
51	$1,196,112	$59,806	$44,584	$0	$0	$0	$1,300,501
52	$1,300,501	$65,025	$45,030	$0	$0	$0	$1,410,556
53	$1,410,556	$70,528	$45,480	$0	$0	$0	$1,526,564
54	$1,526,564	$76,328	$45,935	$0	$0	$0	$1,648,827
55	$1,648,827	$65,953	$0	$85,307	$0	$85,307	$1,629,472
56	$1,629,472	$65,179	$0	$87,014	$0	$87,014	$1,607,637
57	$1,607,637	$64,305	$0	$88,754	$0	$88,754	$1,583,189
58	$1,583,189	$63,328	$0	$90,529	$0	$90,529	$1,555,988
59	$1,555,988	$62,240	$0	$92,340	$0	$92,340	$1,525,888
60	$1,525,888	$61,036	$0	$94,186	$0	$94,186	$1,492,737
61	$1,492,737	$59,709	$0	$96,070	$0	$96,070	$1,456,376
62	$1,456,376	$58,255	$0	$97,991	$0	$97,991	$1,416,640
63	$1,416,640	$56,666	$0	$99,951	$0	$99,951	$1,373,354
64	$1,373,354	$54,934	$0	$101,950	$0	$101,950	$1,326,338
65	$1,326,338	$53,054	$0	$103,989	$26,400	$77,589	$1,301,802
66	$1,301,802	$52,072	$0	$106,069	$26,400	$79,669	$1,274,205
83	$256,910	$10,276	$0	$148,522	$26,400	$122,122	$145,065
84	$145,065	$5,803	$0	$151,493	$26,400	$125,093	$25,774
85	$25,774	$1,031	$0	$154,523	$26,400	$0	$0
86	$0	$0	$0	$157,613	$26,400	$0	$0
87	$0	$0	$0	$160,766	$26,400	$0	$0
88	$0	$0	$0	$163,981	$26,400	$0	$0
89	$0	$0	$0	$167,260	$26,400	$0	$0
90	$0	$0	$0	$170,605	$26,400	$0	$0

Figure 11: Retirement Planner Tool – Detailed Report

Once we found a model that met the plan and that we were comfortable with, we used it as a baseline. At the end of each working year, we tracked whether our retirement nest egg was growing on target. At the beginning of each year, we would adjust some of the input parameters based on actual data from the previous year and regenerate the plan. We updated the "current retirement savings" parameter to reflect the actual ending balance of our investments from the previous year as well as the "percent of income at retirement" parameter based on our annual spending patterns. So year by year, we tracked how we were doing as we crept closer to our final goal.

To our surprise, we found that we were reaching that target much sooner than anticipated. Originally our plan was to retire at age 55. This was the typical target age for early retirement as promoted by the banks and other financial institutions, so we had chosen it as our benchmark.

Once we stopped guessing at the right retirement age and started putting hard numbers behind our estimates, we realized that we might not need to wait that long after all. It eventually got to a point where we had to make the decision of whether working an extra year to pad our total investment was worth it to us or not. We were weighing risks versus rewards. We decided that enduring another year of work-related stress was not worth the incremental savings we could accumulate. The final factor that sealed our decision was the realization that if we wanted to spend quality time with our aging parents, the time was now.

Retirement Planning Spreadsheet

There are a few Old Age Security and Canada Pension Plan situations that the online tool currently does not fully support:

- If you retire before 65, the tool assumes that you will take CPP at age 65 as opposed to potentially choosing another age ranging from 60 to 70.
- Old Age Security rules changed in 2012 so that Canadians younger than age 57 will not receive OAS payments until age 67 as opposed to the previous age of 65. The online tool does not yet reflect this change and so the results are slightly skewed.

We replicated the calculations from this planner in a spreadsheet in order to have more flexibility and control over such variables. Most of the calculations are driven by the parameters specified in the top section of the spreadsheet.

The spreadsheet we created does not automatically account for changes in the age parameters. Instead, it adds one row for each year between the current age and the age just prior to retirement, and one row per year for each of the retirement years. The formulas shift from "savings mode" to "spending mode" in the year of retirement. To adjust the age of retirement, we simply added or deleted rows prior to the row containing the spending formulas. We applied the savings formulas to any new rows by highlighting all the columns from a previous row and dragging, but we had to be careful not to drag columns into the retirement age row, or the spending formulas would be wiped out.

We manually selected the starting age for OAS and CPP by specifying the desired row in the spreadsheet to start including those income sources. Different scenarios were compared by copying the entire contents of the worksheet into new worksheets and adjusting the starting row for CPP. We looked at the impacts of starting CPP payments at age 60 through 70 instead of 65. The monthly amount for CPP would also increase or decrease depending on when we decided we will take it. Currently neither the spreadsheet nor the online tool handles the scenario where each spouse takes CPP at a different age. The spreadsheet could easily be modified to reflect the situation where each spouse takes CPP at a different age. This can be accomplished by including only the first person's CPP payout in the row representing the first age and then adding the second person's CPP payout in the row representing the second age. We did not bother with these changes since we both plan to take CPP at the same age.

We added a few additional features to the spreadsheet. We made a column to enter the actual ending balance at the end of each year so that the next year starts with a more realistic figure than the one provided by the estimates and extrapolations. We also added a column for entering the actual investment contribution amounts for a year, so that the actual growth or rate of return can be calculated. This helped us monitor whether the specified growth parameters that we picked were realistic.

The formulas used in the spreadsheet are shown in Figure 12. The input parameters specified at the top are used in the calculations. As these parameters change, the report below recalculates. The arrows indicate that the formulas just repeat in sequence.

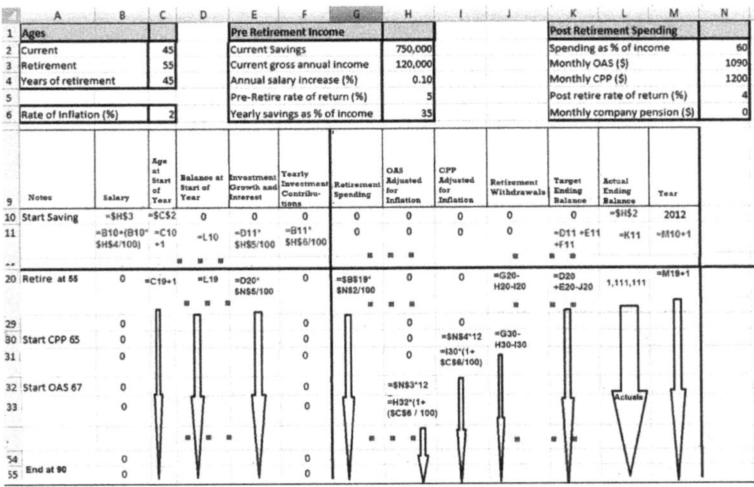

	A		C		E		H		K		N
1	Ages				Pre Retirement Income				Post Retirement Spending		
2	Current		45		Current Savings		750,000		Spending as % of income		60
3	Retirement		55		Current gross annual income		120,000		Monthly OAS ($)		1090
4	Years of retirement		45		Annual salary increase (%)		0.10		Monthly CPP ($)		1200
5					Pre-Retire rate of return (%)		5		Post retire rate of return (%)		4
6	Rate of Inflation (%)		2		Yearly savings as % of income		35		Monthly company pension ($)		0

9	Notes	Salary	Age at Start of Year	Balance at Start of Year	Investment Growth and Interest	Yearly Investment Contributions	Retirement Spending	OAS Adjusted for Inflation	CPP Adjusted for Inflation	Retirement Withdrawals	Target Ending Balance	Actual Ending Balance	Year
10	Start Saving	=$H$3	=$C$2	0	0	0	0	0	0	0	0	=$H$2	2012
11		=B10+(B10*$H$4/100)	=C10+1	=L10	=D11*$H$5/100	=B11*$H$6/100	0	0	0	0	=D11+E11+F11	=K11	=M10+1
20	Retire at 55	0	=C19+1	=L19	=D20*$N$5/100	0	=$B$19*$N$2/100	0	0	=G20-H20-I20	=D20+E20-J20	1,111,111	=M19+1
29		0				0		0	0				
30	Start CPP 65	0				0		0	=$N$4*12	=G30-H30-I30			
31		0				0		0	=I30*(1+$C$6/100)				
32	Start OAS 67	0				0		=$N$3*12					
33		0				0		=H32*(1+($C$6 / 100)				Actuals	
54		0				0							
55	End at 90	0				0							

Figure 12: Retirement Planner Spreadsheet – Formulas

In the retirement report, each row represents a year. The formulas are different for the saving years (pre-retirement) as opposed to the spending years (post-retirement).

The formulas for the saving years:

Column	Column Name	Description	Sample Formula
B	Salary	The starting salary (in cell B10) is taken from cell H3 and then increments in each subsequent year by the percentage of salary increase (cell H4)	=$H$3 =B10*$H$4/ 100
C	Age at Start of Year	The starting age (cell C10) is taken from cell C2 and increments by 1 for each subsequent year	=$C$2 =C10+1
D	Balance at Start of Year	The starting balance for the year is taken from the actual ending balance from previous year, found in column L	=L10
E	Investment Growth and Interest	The investment growth for the year is calculated by taking the starting balance in column D and multiplying by the pre-retirement rate of growth (cell H5)	=D11*$H$5/ 100
F	Yearly Investment Contributions	The annual contribution to retirement savings is calculated by taking the current income in column B and multiplying by the percentage of income that is to be allocated for savings (cell H6)	=B11*$H$6/ 100

G to J	Multiple	These columns are not relevant during the savings years	N/A
K	Target End Balance	Sum of the balance at the start of the year plus the estimated yearly investment growth plus the estimated yearly contributions	=D11+E11+F 11
L	Actual End Balance	Entered at the end of the year based actual investment growth and contributions	Manually entered
M	Year	Informational only; enter the first year and then increment by one for each subsequent year	=M10+1

The formulas for the spending years:

Col.	Column Name	Description	Sample Formula
B	Salary	Zero — no more salary after retirement	0
C	Age at Start of Year	Age increments by 1 for each subsequent year	=C19+1
D	Balance at Start of Year	The starting balance for the year is taken from the actual ending balance from previous year, found in column L	=L19
E	Investment Growth and Interest	The investment growth for the year is calculated by taking the starting balance in column D and multiplying by	=D19*$N$5/100

		the post-retirement percentage growth (cell N5)	
F	Yearly Investment Contributions	Zero — assume no more new investment contributions after retirement	0
G	Retirement Spending	Starts as a percentage of the last pre-retirement salary and adjusted by the inflation factor (C6) each year	=G19*$C$6/100
H	OAS	The specified monthly OAS for the couple (N3) multiplied by 12 for the first year and then adjusted by the inflation factor (C6) each subsequent year Start adding OAS at age 67 for the couple	=$N$3*12 =H33*(1+($C$6/ 100))
I	CPP	Specified monthly CPP for the couple (N4) multiplied by 12 for the year and then adjusted by the inflation factor (C6) each year Start adding CPP at the desired age (between 60 and 70) for the couple If each spouse wants	=$N$4*12 =I31*(1+($C$6/ 100))

		to take CPP at a different age, separate the value in cell N4 into two different cells and start applying at each desired age	
J	Investment Withdrawal	Retired Spending minus OAS minus CPP	=G20-H20-I20
K	Target End Balance	Balance at the start of the year plus the estimated yearly investment growth minus investment withdrawal	=D20+E20-J20
L	Actual End Balance	Entered at the end of the year based actual investment growth and contributions	Manually entered
M	Year	Informational only; enter the first year and then increment by one for each subsequent year	=M19+1

Using the same input parameters, the results on the spreadsheet were made to match the results of the tool to ensure the formulas were accurately applied. (See Figure 13.)

Both the online Globe Investor calculator and the spreadsheet treat the entire retirement investment nest egg as one lump sum without differentiating the split of savings between the various types of accounts such as RRIFs, LIFs, TFSAs and non-registered accounts. Later on, when we looked into how to withdraw money for savings (see the section "Models for Collapsing Investment Accounts"), we created another spreadsheet that took these accounts and their potentially different growth rates into consideration.

Ages	
Current	45
Retirement	55
Years of retirement	45
Rate of Inflation (%)	2

Pre Retirement Income	
Current Savings	750,000
Current gross annual income	120,000
Annual salary increase (%)	0.10
Pre-Retire rate of return (%)	5
Yearly savings as % of income	35

Post Retirement Spending	
Spending as % of income	60
Monthly OAS ($)	1090
Monthly CPP ($)	1200
Post retire rate of return (%)	4
Monthly company pension ($)	0

Actual Retirement Contribution	Actual Growth	Actual % Growth or Rate of Return
50,000	29,542	4

Notes	Salary	Age at Start of Year	Balance at Start of Year	Investment Growth and Interest	Yearly Investment Contributions	Retirement Spending	OAS Adjusted for Inflation	CPP Adjusted for Inflation	Investment Withdrawal	Target Ending Balance	Actual Ending Balance	Year
Starting Year	120,000	45	0	0	0	0	0		0	0	750,000	2012
	120,120	46	750,000	37,500	42,042	0	0		0	829,542	829,542	2013
					⋮	⋮						
	120,963	53	1,398,592	69,930	42,337	0	0		0	1,510,859	1,510,859	2020
	121,084	54	1,510,859	75,543	42,379	0	0		0	1,628,782	1,628,782	2021
Retire	0	55	1,628,782	65,151	0	72,650	0	0	72,650	1,621,283	1,621,283	2022
	0	56	1,621,283	64,851	0	74,103	0	0	74,103	1,612,031	1,612,031	2023
	0	57	1,612,031	64,481	0	75,585	0	0	75,585	1,600,927	1,600,927	2024
					⋮	⋮						
	0	64	1,489,257	59,570	0	86,823	0	0	86,823	1,462,004	1,462,004	2031
Start CPP 65	0	65	1,462,004	58,480	0	88,559	0	14,400	74,159	1,446,325	1,446,325	2032
	0	66	1,446,325	57,853	0	90,330	0	14,688	75,642	1,428,536	1,428,536	2033
Start OAS 67	0	67	1,428,536	57,141	0	92,137	13,080	14,982	64,075	1,421,602	1,421,602	2034
	0	68	1,421,602	56,864	0	93,980	13,342	15,282	65,356	1,413,110	1,413,110	2035
	0	69	1,413,110	56,524	0	95,860	13,609	15,588	66,663	1,402,971	1,402,971	2036
	0	70	1,402,971	56,119	0	97,777	13,881	15,900	67,996	1,391,094	1,391,094	2037
	0	71	1.391.094	55,644	0	99.733	14.159	16.218	69.356	1.377.382	1.377.382	2038
					⋮	⋮						
	0	88	810,535	32,421	0	139,650	19,827	22,708	97,115	745,841	745,841	2055
	0	89	745,841	29,834	0	142,443	20,224	23,162	99,057	676,618	676,618	2056
	0	90	676,618	27,065	0	145,292	20,628	23,625	101,039	602,644	602,644	2057

Figure 13: Retirement Planner Spreadsheet – Inputs and Detailed Report

Saving for Retirement

Once we paid off our mortgage and started seriously saving for retirement, we adhered to the following guiding principles that reflected our shared philosophy about money and spending. We would try to do the following:

1. Live within our means and spend money on only what we could afford
2. Pay as much as possible using credit cards to gain loyalty rewards (cash back, travel miles) but always pay off the monthly bill
3. Find the right balance between spending to enjoy the present and saving for the future

We already had a good base, since we both realized early on the value of saving even a little bit of spare income towards retirement. We each opened RRSPs right off the bat after getting our first jobs after university, and tried to contribute enough to avoid paying income tax or to even get a tax refund. Then we let the power of compound returns work its magic over the years.

Aiding our ability to save and meet our early retirement goals was the fact that we did not have expensive tastes or the desire for lavish lifestyles. We do not own multiple expensive cars but share a single modestly priced vehicle. We do not own a mansion home, summer cottage, boat, designer clothes, valuable jewellery or furs. We don't participate in expensive hobbies like golf, downhill skiing or yachting. Not having children to feed or clothe definitely made a difference in our ability to save. Our major spending vices are travel, theatre and dining out at nice restaurants, but we keep principle number one in mind and spend within our budget.

It's not that we would not have enjoyed all those other things. They were just not high on our priority list, and we did not feel that we were sacrificing to do without them. Saving and spending always has to do with opportunity costs and weighing what is more important to you. We were still able to do all the things that we really enjoyed in the present, while aggressively saving for that future utopia when we no longer had to be slaves to a job. Buying that expensive sports car or cottage could delay our retirement by many years, so we asked ourselves, "Is it worth it?" before making any major expenditure.

Do-It-Yourself Investing

One of the best things that we did, which significantly helped accelerate our ability to retire early, was to learn how to take over the management of our investment portfolio ourselves.

Why We Did It

We previously had our money invested with a financial advisor associated with a bank. During this period, we had very little understanding about the concepts of investing, where our money was invested, how it was doing, and what value we were getting for the fees we were paying to the advisor.

We started to learn more about topics like MERs (management expense ratios for investment products), mutual funds, exchange-traded funds (ETFs) and tips for picking stocks as we read the business section of the *Globe and Mail*. We began to realize that our financial advisor had placed us in mutual funds that had relatively high fees and seemed to be resting on his laurels and doing little else for us from year to year. On top of that, our portfolio was not even performing as well as the TSX index.

We also began to question the real value and motivation around the financial advisor's role in general. We came to the conclusion that in some, if not most, cases, the job was actually more of a salesperson than that of an "advisor." Our financial advisor's main purpose was to sell products for his company and make his living by generating commissions. Whether those products were in our best interests seemed to be a secondary consideration, since this was not what he was compensated on. He received a percentage of our portfolio (the management fee), whether he did any work managing it or not, and whether it was profitable or not. If our portfolio value actually increased through natural market growth, our advisor got more and more money without necessarily doing any more work. He was also paid a commission on the funds that he sold us, so it was most profitable for him to put us in funds that had the highest fees. Each year, we had to pay our financial advisor a flat fee plus his commissions on mutual fund management fees, even when he lost money for us.

We basically met with our advisor only once a year at portfolio review time. He would provide us with reports and charts that we didn't totally understand, which is not a good feeling to have. We tried for several years during these meetings to convince our advisor to look for funds with lower fees for us to move to, but he kept insisting he had us in the best possible position. We suggested ETFs, but he declared that mutual funds would outperform them. (ETFs are now widely recognized as a viable way to reduce fees.) We suggested moving into stocks, but he threw it back on us, saying, "Okay, but you tell me which ones." Isn't that what we were we were paying him for? Eventually, getting fed up and after doing some more research, we decided to take a leap of faith and try to manage our investments by ourselves. The way we figured it, no one would spend as much time monitoring our portfolio or would care about its performance as much as we would.

It soon became clear that doing it ourselves would not be as difficult as we had initially feared. There is so much information and advice available these days in books and newspapers and, especially, on the Internet to help us get up to speed. The added benefit was that we were totally engaged and had a full understanding of our own portfolio and how it was doing.

The final kicker that convinced us we did the right thing was when we heard that a former colleague who used to be in equipment sales had suddenly become a financial advisor — if he could do it, so could we. We were at least as qualified (or as unqualified) as he was!

And one final story: The day we informed our former financial advisor that we were leaving and taking all our money with us, he suddenly thought of several new mutual funds on the market that could help reduce our fees. It was a case of too little, too late.

I'm sure there are many financial advisors out there who do a much better job than ours did. But as it turns out, having this bad experience was the best thing that ever happened to us. It gave us the courage and impetus to take control of our own destiny, as opposed to ignorantly leaving it in the hands of a third party.

How We Did It

Research

We began our research by reviewing many different sources, including financial and investment books, business sections in newspapers, and magazines. Some important references that provided us with a solid foundation for our knowledge included the book *Money Management For Canadians All-in-One Desk Reference For Dummies*, the business section of the *Globe and Mail* newspaper, and *MoneySense* magazine.

Of course, the Internet was an invaluable fountain of information. We found websites that provide statistics and historical performance data on stocks and bonds, investment strategies, retirement and tax calculators. The Service Canada website contains information about government programs and services, including the Canada Pension Plan (CPP) and Old Age Security (OAS), which are of particular importance to retirees.

We also watched the dedicated investment television channel Business News Network (BNN), which provides investment news, advice and updates seemingly around the clock. This station is always offered on the TVs at the gym, so we could learn as we exercised.

A full list of sources and websites can be found in the last chapter, "References."

Online Discount Brokerage – Scotia iTRADE

We took all our money and transferred it into an online discount brokerage service for self-directed investing. We created the same personal RRSPs, spousal RRSP and non-registered accounts that we had with our previous financial institution and transferred all the stocks, bonds and funds in kind. Once everything was moved over, we reviewed each asset in our portfolio and rebalanced to fit our retirement investment strategy (see the section of the same name).

At the time of our financial move, in 2005, one of the cheapest discount brokerage options was E*TRADE Canada. This company was offering fees of $9.99 a trade for accounts of value greater than $50,000. The fees for most other brokerage firms were in the $19.99 to $39.99 range. Since then, Scotiabank has bought out E*TRADE and rebranded it as Scotia iTRADE, and all the other brokerage firms had to lower their fees to compete. Currently, I'm not sure if there is that much difference among the various discount brokerages, but we've stayed with Scotia iTRADE since it is a big hassle to move the funds around without a good reason to do so. Scotia iTRADE meets all our financial needs for investing and trading and provides good, knowledgeable customer service over the phone.

Scotia iTRADE provides all the online tools required to manage our accounts, to track their performances, to tie them to our bank account so we can easily make contributions or withdrawals, and most important, to be able to buy and sell bonds and mutual funds and trade stocks on the Canadian and US stock exchanges. (See Figure 14.)

The interface for trading stocks allows us to make a "limit" buy or sell, rather than trading at the market price. There are many websites, including Scotia iTRADE, that provide historical prices for a stock over periods of anywhere from a day to 10 or more years. As we watched the prices of stocks over a period of time, we noticed that they usually go through a peak or valley to reach a high or low. This seemed true even throughout a single day of trading. Using a "limit order" (an order type that sets the maximum or minimum price at which you are willing to buy or sell a particular stock) allows us to guess at what that price will be, in the eternal fool's game of trying to buy low and sell high. We can keep a buy or sell order active for the day or up to a month while we wait for our price to hit.

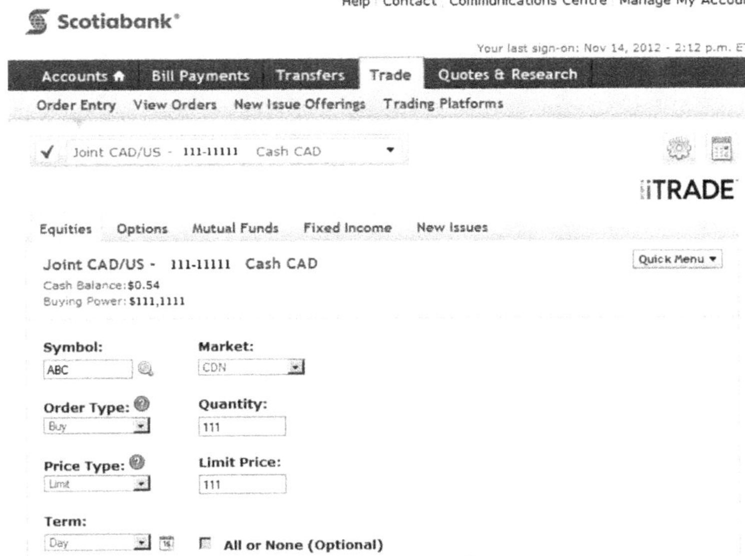

Figure 14: Scotia iTRADE – Stock Trade Interface

Accounts in Scotia iTRADE

Scotia iTRADE supports all the types of accounts that you might want to own during both the savings and the retirement (income payout) phases. (See Figure 15.)

During the savings phase, we contributed to the following accounts:

- Personal Registered Retirement Savings Plan (RRSP) account for each of us.
- Spousal RRSP to help balance income between us for tax purposes.
- Tax-Free Savings Account (TFSA) for each of us.
- Canadian joint non-registered account for any additional savings after contributing to the registered accounts — we

made this a joint account so that we could balance income between us for tax purposes.

- US joint non-registered account — we bought a small amount of US stock with this account so that we could generate US dividends that we then transfer into a US bank account; this gives us access to some US cash for travel purposes without having to pay currency exchange rates or fees. We kept the amount low because foreign stocks do not qualify for the dividend tax credit and will be taxed at the same rate as employment income in this account. We purchased larger amounts of foreign stock within our RRSPs, which were tax-sheltered.

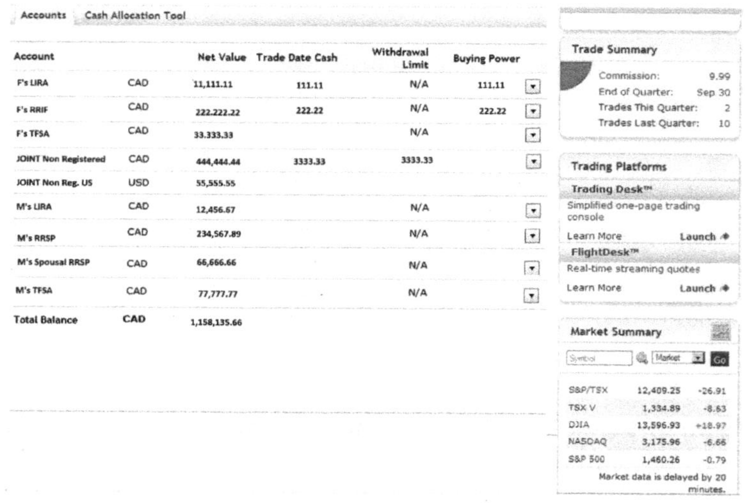

Accounts Cash Allocation Tool

Account		Net Value	Trade Date Cash	Withdrawal Limit	Buying Power
F's LIRA	CAD	11,111.11	111.11	N/A	111.11
F's RRIF	CAD	222.222.22	222.22	N/A	222.22
F's TFSA	CAD	33.333.33		N/A	
JOINT Non Registered	CAD	444,444.44	3333.33	3333.33	
JOINT Non Reg. US	USD	55,555.55			
M's LIRA	CAD	12,456.67		N/A	
M's RRSP	CAD	234,567.89		N/A	
M's Spousal RRSP	CAD	66,666.66		N/A	
M's TFSA	CAD	77,777.77		N/A	
Total Balance	CAD	1,158,135.66			

Figure 15: Scotia iTRADE – Investment Accounts

Once we entered the retirement phase, we created or converted to the following accounts to prepare for receiving income flow from our investments:

- Registered Retirement Income Fund (RRIF) to transfer our RRSPs into so that we can collapse them and start receiving income from them
- Locked-in Retirement Account (LIRA) for each of us, into which we transferred our respective company-defined contribution accumulations; these cannot be collapsed or accessed until we reach at least age 55

Portfolio Monitoring

Recently, Scotia iTRADE has been adding more and more analysis and tracking tools to help its users manage their portfolios, but they were not as available when we first started out. Instead, we found that the *Globe and Mail*'s online investment tools, including their "My Watchlist" met our needs. To create a watchlist, we signed up for an account with the *Globe and Mail* website and then accessed this link: www.theglobeandmail.com/globe-investor/my-watchlist.

A watchlist allows us to add stocks to it and choose or configure what criteria it keeps track of. We can select from preset views related to criteria such as dividends, earnings, news articles about the stock, or percentage performance over different time durations. There is a view called "My Shares" that allows us to put in the number of shares that we own in each stock so that it tracks the current value of the holding based on the up-to-the-minute stock price. Other views provided include ones called "Overview," "Ratios," "Dividends," "Earnings," "All News," "Per Cent Performance" and "My Alerts." Or we can choose to build our own view, selecting from over 50 different criteria, which we did. (See Figure 16.)

Ticker	Company	Latest Price	Chg Today	Chg Today %	Yield	Dividend Per Share	Analyst Recommendation	PE Ratio	Target Price	YTD Chg %	52-Week Range
BCE-T	BCE Inc.	42.15	0.03	0.07%	5.39%	$ 2.27	Hold	13.60	$ 44.13	-0.75%	39.12 - 45.28
BNS-T	Bank of Nova S	54.50	0.02	0.04%	4.18%	$ 2.28	Buy	10.52	$ 60.18	7.22%	47.54 - 57.17
CM-T	CIBC	79.80	0.75	0.95%	4.71%	$ 3.76	Hold	10.31	$ 84.00	8.14%	68.15 - 79.43
CNR-T	Canadian Natio	87.36	0.24	0.28%	1.72%	$ 1.50	Hold	14.39	$ 95.17	9.00%	74.22 - 92.20
RY-T	Royal Bank of (	57.95	0.14	0.24%	4.14%	$ 2.40	Hold	12.10	$ 60.46	11.49%	43.30 - 59.13
RY.PR.D-T	Royal Bank of (	25.90	0.04	0.15%	4.36%	$ 1.13	Hold	12.10	$ --	-0.08%	25.06 - 26.39
SLF-T	Sun Life Financ	27.15	0.05	0.18%	5.30%	$ 1.44	Hold	--	$ 25.23	43.65%	17.92 - 27.21
T-N	AT&T Inc.	34.36	0.51	1.51%	5.24%	$ 1.80	Hold	14.87	$ 36.92	13.62%	27.41 - 38.58
T-T	TELUS Corp.	64.98	0.29	0.45%	3.94%	$ 2.56	Buy	9.82	$ 68.10	12.73%	52.76 - 65.79
TD-T	TD Bank	81.40	0.41	0.51%	3.78%	$ 3.08	Strong Buy	11.90	$ 92.54	6.70%	68.13 - 85.65
TRI-T	Thomson Reut(	27.31	0.14	0.52%	4.67%	$ 1.28	Hold	--	$ 31.15	0.29%	26.10 - 30.25
TRP-T	TransCanada C	45.36	0.11	0.24%	3.88%	$ 1.76	Buy	23.38	$ 48.17	1.86%	40.34 - 46.29

Figure 16: *Globe and Mail* Watchlists

Our customized "My Watchlist" view tracks the following criteria in order to help us monitor the health of our portfolio:

- Stock ticker symbol
- Company name
- Latest price
- Daily change in value based on dollars
- Daily change in value based on percentage
- Dividend payout per share
- Dividend yield (calculated as dividend payout divided by current price)
- Analyst recommendations — an average of the buy/hold/sell recommendation from multiple analysts who rate the stock
- YTD change in price by percentage
- Total rate of return in one year
- Target price estimated by analysts
- 52-week low to high price range
- Price-to-earnings ratio
- Latest news about the stock
- Market capitalization in millions of dollars (10,000+ = large cap; 1000–9999 =mid cap; < 1000 = small cap)
- Percentage dividend growth over five years
- Percentage of stock price paid out as dividends
- Next ex-dividend date or ex-date — the purchase transaction of stocks needs to be completed before this date in order to qualify for the next dividend
- Next dividend payout date

As we continued to build up our portfolio, we created different watchlists for different tracking purposes, including the following:

- Total stocks we currently owned
- Target portfolio that we wanted at retirement
- Stocks by account types (RRSP, non-registered, TFSA, etc.)
- Stocks to keep an eye on and consider purchasing
- Stocks by market capitalization (small cap, mid cap, large cap)

From the watchlist, we can drill down to get more information on each stock, including a chart of the share price movements over a one-month period, a breakdown of analyst recommendations, company financials, news headlines, a list of competitors with comparative statistics, earnings and estimates, trends and revisions.

Investment Tracking Spreadsheet

We created a spreadsheet to track each stock purchase that we made per account, taking note of the date, quantity, price and value of the purchase. We also kept track of the date, price and amount of any stock sales. This information is important especially for our non-registered account since it is needed for tax purposes to calculate capital losses or gains upon the sale of the stock. The spreadsheet also calculates the expected amount of dividend that would be paid for each stock in each account, and keeps track of the frequency of payment and the next expected payment date. (See Figure 17.) This will be useful for determining the timing and amount of income flow during the retirement years. We also wanted to confirm on a regular basis that we would be receiving the expected dividend amounts and that they would be paid out around the time frame when they will be expected.

Account	Sector	Stock	Buy Date	Buy Price	Quant	Buy Value	Current Value	Yield per Shr	Div Yield %	Market Cap	Current Price	Payout Frequency	Total Payout	Reg Payout	Pay Date	Target Yearly Dividend	Apr Jul Oct	May Aug Nov	Jun Sep Dec
RRSP	Finance	ABC	28-Feb-2011	35.48	574	20,366	24,286	2.27	6.37	LARGE	42.31	Jan Apr Jul Oct	1,302.98	325.75	Jan 15 as of Dec 13th	1,302.98	325.75		
	REIT	DEF	28-Sep-2011	19.9	2150	42,785	56,330	1.62	6.18	SMALL	26.2	Monthly	3,483.00	290.26	**Nov 15 as of Oct 28**	3,483.00	290.25	290.25	290.25
TFSA	Telco	GHI	08-Feb-2010 19-Jul-2011 10-Jan-2011	13.2 15.15 13.82	700 68 498	16,448	21,560	1.18	6.66	LARGE	17.73	Jan Apr Jul Oct	1,434.88	358.72	Jan 15 as of Dec 28	1,434.83	358.72		
Non Registered	Utilities	HU	10-Jul-2012	16.84	5,027	84,655	84,152	0.82	4.62	MID	16.74	Monthly	4,122.14	343.51	Dec 10 as of Nov 4				
	Retail	KLM	30-Jan-2012 22-Mar-2012	14.48 23.2	2118 1320	61,293	80,662	1.44	6.15	MID	23.43	Monthly	4,950.72	412.56	**Nov 15 as of Oct 28**	4,950.72	412.66	412.56	412.56
	Manufact.	NOP	15-Sep-2011	20	69	1,380	1,736	0.72	2.86	MID	25.16	Monthly	49.68	4.14	**Nov 15 as of Oct 28**	49.68	4.14	4.14	4.14
	Transport	QRS	22-Sep-2011	27.92	2450	68404	85750	1.76	5.03	LARGE	35.00	Feb May Aug Nov	4,312.00	1,078.00	Feb 1 as of Jan 7	4,312.00		1,078.00	
	Finance	TUV	25-Jun-2012	14.94	282	4,213	4,219	0.54	3.61	LARGE	14.96	Monthly	152.28	12.69	Mar 5 as of Feb 4	152.28	12.69	12.69	12.69
	Finance	AAA	13-Jan-2012	78	1370	106,860	118,217	1.50	1.74	LARGE	86.29	Mar Jun Sep Dec	2,055.00	513.75	Dec 30 as of Nov 7	2,055.00			513.75

Figure 17: Investment Tracking Spreadsheet by Account

The spreadsheet is also used to calculate the sum total value of each stock across all the accounts. During our savings period, both the current total and the target total were tracked in order to determine how much more of each stock was to be purchased. Using data filters, this summary allowed us to verify the current and target dollar values that we owned in each stock, market sector and market capitalization to ensure we did not exceed our risk tolerance maximums that we set for ourselves.

This summary view also projects the target amount of dividends that we will receive each month or quarter, so that we can determine when we have enough income flow to meet our expenses.

Finally, on a regular basis we check in on the dividend payout per share and dividend yield to see if any of our stocks have reduced their dividend, thus affecting our expected income payments. (See Figure 18.)

Retirement Investment Strategy

Once we were managing our own investment portfolio, we needed a strategy for building it into a steady, sustainable source of income that would fund our retirement years.

TOTALS BY STOCK = Sum of all Accounts for a Given Stock Filter by Sector, Market Cap, More to Buy																					
Extra Shares to Buy	Value still to buy	Sector	Stock Ticker	Target Amt	Current Quantity	Target Value	Current Value	$ Yield per Shr	Div Yield %	Market Cap	Current Price	Total Earnings	Yearly Payout Total	Actual Payout	Pay Date	Target Quantity by Stock	Target Value by Stock	Target Yearly Dividend	Jan Apr Jul Oct	Feb May Aug Nov	Mar Jun Sep Dec
2,249	33,960	REIT	AAA	2,649	400	40,000	6,040	0.80	5.30	MID	15.10	Monthly	320	26.67	Dec 31 as of Nov 28	2,649	40,000	2119.21	176.60	176.60	176.60
500	5,000	Retail	BBB	1,000	500	10,000	5,000	0.45	4.50	SMALL	10.00	Monthly	225	18.75	Dec 31 as of Nov 2	1,000	10,000	450.00	37.50	37.50	37.50
500	5,000	Financial	CCC	1,000	500	10,000	5,000	0.45	4.50	LARGE	10.00	Jan Apr Jul Oct	225	18.75	Jan 1 as of Nov 3	1,000	10,000	450.00	112.50		
500	5,000	Financial	DDD	1,000	500	10,000	5,000	0.45	4.50	LARGE	10.00	Jan Apr Jul Oct	225	18.75	Jan 31 as of Nov 4	1,000	10,000	450.00		112.50	
500	5,000	Financial	EEE	1,000	500	10,000	5,000	0.45	4.50	LARGE	10.00	Feb May Aug Nov	225	18.75	Feb 5 as of Jan 5	1,000	10,000	450.00		112.50	
500	5,000	Transport	FFF	1,000	500	10,000	5,000	0.45	4.50	LARGE	10.00	Feb May Aug Nov	225	18.75	Feb 5 as of Jan 6	1,000	10,000	450.00		112.50	
500	5,000	Utilities	GGG	1,000	500	10,000	5,000	0.45	4.50	MID	10.00	Feb May Aug Nov	225	18.75	Feb 5 as of Jan 7	1,000	10,000	450.00		112.50	
500	5,000	Entertain	HHH	1,000	500	10,000	5,000	0.45	4.50	MID	10.00	Feb May Aug Nov	225	18.75	Feb 5 as of Jan 8	1,000	10,000	450.00		112.50	
500	5,000	Retail	III	1,000	500	10,000	5,000	0.45	4.50	MID	10.00	Feb May Aug Nov	225	18.75	Feb 5 as of Jan 9	1,000	10,000	450.00		112.50	
500	5,000	Oil & Gas	JJJ	1,000	500	10,000	5,000	0.45	4.50	MID	10.00	Feb May Aug Nov	225	18.75	Feb 5 as of Jan 10	1,000	10,000	450.00		112.50	
500	5,000	Manufact	KKK	1,000	500	10,000	5,000	0.45	4.50	SMALL	10.00	Feb May Aug Nov	225	18.75	Feb 5 as of Jan 11	1,000	10,000	450.00		112.50	
500	5,000	Telco	MMM	1,000	500	10,000	5,000	0.45	4.50	LARGE	10.00	Feb May Aug Nov	225	18.75	Feb 5 as of Jan 12	1,000	10,000	450.00		112.50	
500	5,000	Oil & Gas	NNN	1,000	500	10,000	5,000	0.45	4.50	MID	10.00	Feb May Aug Nov	225	18.75	Feb 5 as of Jan 13	1,000	10,000	450.00		112.50	
500	5,000	REIT	OOO	1,000	500	10,000	5,000	0.45	4.50	MID	10.00	Feb May Aug Nov	225	18.75	Mar 5 as of Feb 14	1,000	10,000	450.00			112.50
483	24,355	Financial	XXX	1,983	1,500	100,000	75,645	2.30	4.56	LARGE	50.43	Jan Apr Jul Oct	3450	862.5	Feb 5 as of Jan 15	1,983	100,000	4560.78	1140.19		

Figure 18: Investment Tracking Spreadsheet by Stock Total Value

It is a given that fixed-income products such as bonds or GICs will provide a guaranteed rate of return and will retain their dollar value, as long as you hold them to maturity. In contrast, stocks will fluctuate in value and could rise or fall depending on a variety of market factors. Therefore, common wisdom dictates that as you get closer to retirement, you need to move to a greater percentage of fixed income and a lower percentage of equities within your portfolio.

This premise assumes that the goal is to generate income from the sale of your stocks or bonds, which depletes your capital during retirement with no way of replenishing it. Fixed income products are also susceptible to the impacts of inflation. A bond will pay a guaranteed fixed amount of income, either at regular intervals or in total at maturity. However, the buying power of that fixed amount could be significantly eroded if inflation is high. Add this to the fact that our turbulent economy since 2008 has caused bond yields to drop to unreasonably low rates, and suddenly the strategy to increase fixed income holdings no longer seems as attractive.

Our strategy was to purchase dividend-bearing stock and accumulate enough to be able to live off the dividends without touching the capital for as long as possible, or at least until age 65 when government pensions like Old Age Security and Canada Pension Plan would kick in. While stock prices rise and fall regularly, dividend payments are not as volatile, especially in strong, well-run companies with good balance sheets. If we could live off our dividends while preserving our capital, then we could weather temporary drops in stock price as long as the companies did not drastically drop their dividends to match. If any company did drop their dividend significantly, we could reduce our spending while looking into the viability of swapping out this stock for another dividend-paying stock that met our purposes.

To reduce risk, we tried to invest in different sectors and looked for blue-chip stocks where possible, especially those with a history of raising dividends, which would help to hedge against inflation. In order to generate a reasonable amount of income without requiring an unachievable amount of capital, we needed our stock to generate a minimum yield of 3.5% while the average yield of all our stocks needed to generate at least 4% or more. This was a fairly conservative growth rate to reflect the turbulent economical times that we've experienced over the past few years and that will probably continue over the next few. Historically, both stocks and bonds have returned a much higher rate, but we could not count on this. We strived to limit our exposure by not having more than 20%–25% in any one sector.

We found that finance, telecommunications, real estate (REITs), transportation and utilities were good sectors to concentrate on. To reach the required average yield, we also needed to add some higher-risk mid cap and small cap stocks to the portfolio. We looked for ones that were highly recommended by market analysts and had strong, profitable balance sheets and a low price-to-earnings ratio, which is a widely used factor for comparing the values of companies.

We tried to keep the distribution of our portfolio so that we had no more than 15% of our value in small cap stocks and 35% in mid cap stocks, with the rest in large cap or fixed-income investments. We spread out our investments across different individual stocks with the aim of having no single stock amounting to more than 5% of our portfolio, while limiting our small cap holdings in any stock to no more than 3%–4%. For example, we thought the big six Canadian banks were good, solid, large cap companies that paid relatively good, steady dividends and had a history of raising those dividends regularly. Instead of choosing one to invest a large sum in, we invested smaller amounts in each of them. With these attempts at diversification, we tried to spread our risk with the assumption that it is unlikely that all our stocks would drastically reduce their dividends at the same time.

Our portfolio consists mainly of Canadian dividend stocks. We considered further diversifying by buying more US stocks, but there were several issues with this. First is the tax consideration. We did not want to buy US stock in our non-registered account since its dividends would be taxed at a higher rate than Canadian dividends. We addressed this by moving any US stock into our RRSPs. The second consideration was the requirement for steady income flow when we retired. The amount of income generated from the payment of US dividends was affected by the additional variable of currency conversion. Therefore, we limited our exposure to US stock.

We also looked at mutual funds and ETFs as a way of further diversifying into sectors, as well as buying into foreign markets that we could not access from the Canadian and US stock exchanges. While these products are good during the savings phase, most of them don't pay out a regular dividend and also charge a management fee. As we got closer to reaching our retirement goals and requiring regular income flow, we sold these and continued to buy Canadian stocks that pay out dividends.

We did have bonds within our RRSPs and were in the process of forming a bond ladder. But then the markets tanked and yields fell to unreasonable rates (some less than what savings accounts were paying) and terms (more than 5–10 years to get more than 1% yield) for securely rated bonds. It became unviable to continue to replace our maturing bonds with new ones since the returns would not even keep up with inflation. Yet in a further attempt to diversify, we did find some bond ETFs that represented groups of bonds in the Canadian, US and foreign markets. These bond funds were paying more than a 3.5% yield, which met our target.

So we had our plan and needed to hunker down to the task of saving. Because we were going after dividends and yield, we continued to buy when the stock prices dropped (buy low!) and were rewarded once recovery began. Our strategy has held up so far, even through the stock crash of 2008 and the turbulent times since. Although our stock prices have bounced up and down like a yo-yo, except for a couple of exceptions, the dividend yields were not lowered. On the contrary, once the markets started to rebound, many of our stocks have actually had their dividend payouts increased.

DRIPs

During the savings phase, we learned through more research that one way to compound growth in our existing stocks while saving the Scotia iTRADE transaction fee of $9.99 per trade was to DRIP eligible stock. DRIP stands for "dividend reinvestment plan" and is supported by most banks and some REITs as well as other companies. The idea is that when a dividend is paid out, instead of paying it to you in cash, the money is automatically reinvested into buying more stock shares. Because the company takes care of this purchase, you are not charged the transaction free from your discount broker. This also means that you do not have to let small amounts of dividend sit idle and not earning in your account until you accumulate enough money to make it worth spending the $9.99 to buy more stock. Some companies even provide a discount (sometimes as much as 2% or more) for stock bought within the DRIP program in order to encourage enrolment.

Obviously, once we reached the retirement phase, we had to "un-DRIP" any stock that we required to start generating dividend income. For accounts like our LIRAs, which we cannot touch until we reach 55, we will stay in the DRIP program to continue to grow our stock value. In fact, we deliberately structured our holdings so that DRIP-eligible stocks would reside in accounts where we do not intend to or cannot draw income from immediately.

Accounting for Inflation

The greatest risk to our retirement strategy is inflation. It is almost a given that throughout the years, inflation will make our expense needs grow. What is unknown is whether our income will grow proportionately to cover the difference. An inflation factor of 2% was included in our retirement calculations, so to some extent, this was accounted for in our planning. Although there will definitely be periods where it is higher, we picked 2% as the average to use over the span of our retirement years since it is the Bank of Canada's target rate.

We also have anticipated revenue increases or expense reductions that will take effect at various stages of retirement.

Since we retired at 48 and cannot access the money in our LIRAs until age 55, we had to make sure we had enough income to support us without this revenue source. At 55 when the LIRAs can be converted to Life Income Funds (LIFs), we will get a planned income boost.

We are currently planning to start receiving Canada Pension Plan benefits at age 65. If it turns out that we urgently need more money by age 60, we can always reconsider this plan and take the CPP early, albeit at a significantly discounted rate. At age 67, we will each qualify for Old Age Security benefits. Both of these pensions are indexed for inflation.

At least some of our stocks will probably raise their dividends over time, thus increasing our revenue stream. When picking stocks, we particularly looked for ones that have a history of raising their dividends and have included some of these in our portfolio.

At age 65, government benefits for seniors kick in that will relieve some of our tax burden, letting us keep more of our gross income. Health benefits that Ontario seniors can access through OHIP, such as the Ontario Drug Benefit (ODB) program, will start to partially cover prescription drugs, dental care, vision care and physiotherapy. As we get older, we will start to incur more medical expenses. In counterbalance, travel, one of the largest line items in our retirement budget, will start to decline. Age will start to slow us down so that we will not be able to travel as long or go as far afield as we did in our younger days. Travel insurance will also start to become prohibitive and will further curtail our trips.

If inflation grows faster than expected, we have some plans for remediation. Obviously, we could start by economizing more and spending less. On top of that, we have a few more contingency plans.

Our strategy was to live on the dividends from our stock, but if that becomes insufficient, we can start to sell the capital. Historically speaking, in the long term stock markets tend to rise. So over time, the value of at least some of our stock should probably be higher. We will try to sell stock that suffered capital loss to offset ones that made capital gains in order to reduce our tax burden.

Unfortunately, selling stock becomes a double whammy since we will not only reduce our investment base but also lose the dividends that those shares would provide. At that point, our strategy will shift from living off the dividends to depending on both dividends and the value of the stock. Hopefully we will not need this option until later on in our retirement so that our capital does not deplete too rapidly.

Because the amounts have been so small so far, we decided not to include the dividends from our TFSAs in our regular revenue stream. Instead, we will use them as emergency money in case a month arises where we have unusually large expenditures that cannot be covered by our cash float. In a later year if there is excess money, we can re-contribute the amount of the withdrawal. All of this can be done tax-free. If the shortfall seems to be chronic, then we can start to include the TFSA dividends as part of our monthly revenue.

Finally, we have not included the value of our home in any of our retirement plans, but it is an asset that can become a revenue source in our later years if required. From selling the home and moving to more economical accommodations to getting a mortgage or reverse mortgage on the home, there are many options that can be used as our final contingency. Selling the home will obviously produce a large amount of capital that could fund the move to a retirement or nursing home. If we want to stay in our home but need more revenue, a mortgage would provide relief, but we would have to start repaying the mortgage immediately, thus depleting this revenue source quicker. A reverse mortgage would also provide us with a large sum of funds, but we would not have to pay any interest as long as we continue to live in the home. Once we move out, due to death or health reasons, the lender would need to be paid back the principal and all interest due. The home would probably have to be sold at that point to cover the debt. We are not counting on requiring this final contingency, but it's good to have a backup plan just in case.

Structuring Retirement Income

While we were saving for retirement, we tried to structure our investments in such a way as to minimize personal income tax and provide the necessary income flow for the retirement years. We read a lot to try to understand the various tax and pension rules in order to determine how we could benefit from what the government offered. This is a never-ending task, since the rules seem to change on a regular basis.

Gross versus Net Income

All our previously described budgets and estimates for retirement spending were based on a net after-tax income. This meant the amount of money we generated from our retirement capital needed to be even higher in order to account for the income tax that we would have to pay. The trick was to figure out how much gross income we would require in order to achieve our target net income. We reviewed various online calculators to try to figure this out. In each case, a new version of the calculator is released each year to reflect the latest tax rates and rules.

One such calculator is provided by LSM Insurance (lsminsurance.ca /calculators/canada/income-tax) and can be used to generate a conservative estimate of the gross income required. We specified a guess for taxable income, and it calculated the tax owed and net income remaining and the average and marginal tax rates for each province. Since we knew our target net income, we kept increasing the taxable income until we reached the expected value under the field marked "After Tax Income" for Ontario.

Because we were income splitting, for estimation purposes we could evenly divide our budgeted net income in two and each of us needed to generate gross income for our half only. As an example, assume we wanted to live on $6000/month or $72,000/year net. According to the 2012 calculator, each of us required gross income of about $43,000 to generate our share of the net income, which was just over $36,000. (See Figure 19.)

The resultant taxable income amount will be higher than actually required, since the calculator does not differentiate type of income and treats all of it as employment income. In reality, the majority of our income will consist of Canadian eligible dividends, which results in a much lower tax burden. Regardless, this provided a good starting point to verifying the real number and included a bit of contingency to make sure we had saved enough.

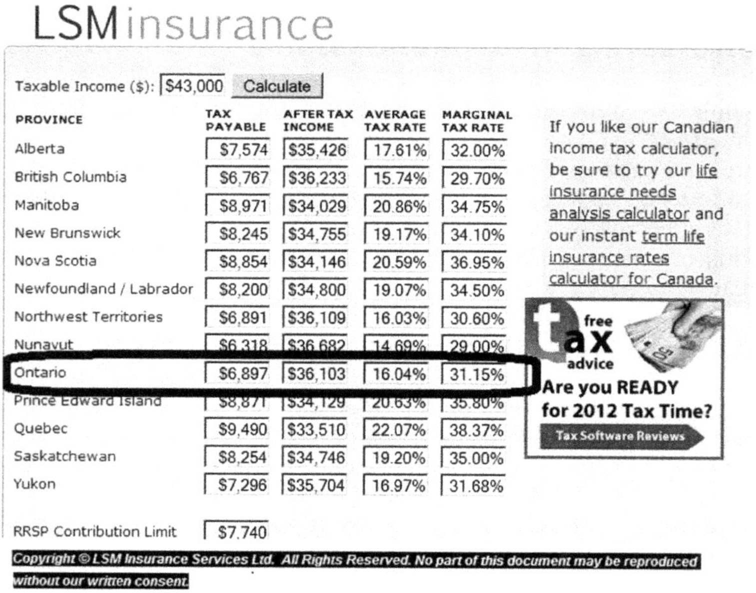

LSMinsurance

Taxable Income ($): $43,000 Calculate

PROVINCE	TAX PAYABLE	AFTER TAX INCOME	AVERAGE TAX RATE	MARGINAL TAX RATE
Alberta	$7,574	$35,426	17.61%	32.00%
British Columbia	$6,767	$36,233	15.74%	29.70%
Manitoba	$8,971	$34,029	20.86%	34.75%
New Brunswick	$8,245	$34,755	19.17%	34.10%
Nova Scotia	$8,854	$34,146	20.59%	36.95%
Newfoundland / Labrador	$8,200	$34,800	19.07%	34.50%
Northwest Territories	$6,891	$36,109	16.03%	30.60%
Nunavut	$6,318	$36,682	14.69%	29.00%
Ontario	$6,897	$36,103	16.04%	31.15%
Prince Edward Island	$8,871	$34,129	20.63%	35.80%
Quebec	$9,490	$33,510	22.07%	38.37%
Saskatchewan	$8,254	$34,746	19.20%	35.00%
Yukon	$7,296	$35,704	16.97%	31.68%

RRSP Contribution Limit $7,740

If you like our Canadian income tax calculator, be sure to try our life insurance needs analysis calculator and our instant term life insurance rates calculator for Canada.

Copyright © LSM Insurance Services Ltd. All Rights Reserved. No part of this document may be reproduced without our written consent.

Figure 19: LSM Insurance – Tax Calculator

Another calculator that results in a more detailed tax estimate based on income sources is provided by Walter Harder & Associates (www.walterharder.ca/T1.asp). With this calculator, we could separately enter our projected Canadian eligible stock dividends from our non-registered account as well as our RRIF income. The favourable tax benefits of Canadian dividend income in the non-registered account would be taken into consideration. (See Figure 20.)

In the example from the previous calculator, $43,000 gross income (all treated as regular income) was required to generate approximately $36,000 net income. With this calculator, splitting the $43,000 into $31,000 dividends and a $12,000 RRIF resulted in net income of $41,523. This was higher than the $36,000 desired net income. The calculator showed that we could generate approximately $36,000 of net income with only $24,600 of dividends and the same $12,000 RRIF income.

This calculator also shows the dividend gross-up and dividend tax credit to further clarify how tax is calculated on Canadian eligible dividends. Note that with this online calculator, the current tax year is offered for a fee but the previous years are free. While the previous years' calculators will not provide the exact answer for the current year, the values will be close enough for estimation and evaluation purposes.

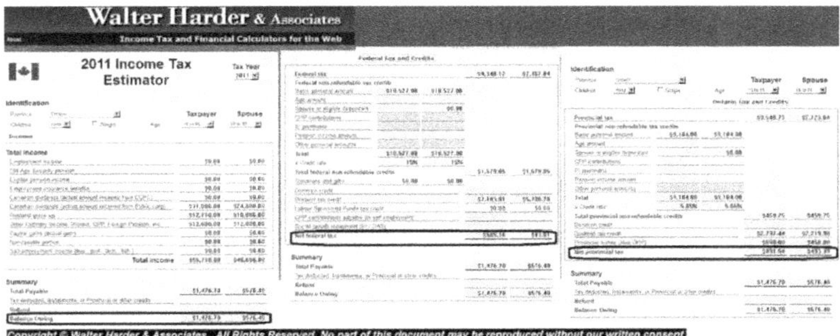

Figure 20: Walter Harder & Associates – Tax Calculator

Minimizing Income Tax

We investigated multiple factors that affected the amount of income tax each of us would owe annually during our retirement. Certain tax impacts were accentuated by our early retirement goals. It would be many years before we would be able to participate in tax advantages geared toward seniors, such as the age amount tax credit or the pension income amount tax credit. Therefore, it was more important than ever that we planned carefully and structured our investment portfolio with tax implications in mind. To accomplish this, we needed to understand the Canadian tax structure.

Income Tax Brackets

Canada has a progressive income tax system that segregates income into tax brackets and taxes the additional income that falls into each higher tax bracket at a higher rate. Figure 21 shows an example of how income in the highest tax bracket is broken up and incrementally taxed at each level. In 2011, the highest federal tax rate was 29% for taxable income exceeding $128,800. But it is not the entire amount that is taxed at that level. The first $41,544 is taxed at only 15%. The next $41,544 is taxed at 22%, and the following $45,712 is taxed at 26%. Only the final $21,200 is taxed at what is called the "marginal tax rate," or the highest rate that your last income dollar will be taxed at. Provincial tax rates follow a similar pattern, although each province sets its own rates and possibly adds additional surtaxes, like Ontario does. The average tax rate, calculated by dividing the total tax paid by the taxable income, is actually only 21.22% in this example.

Many of the strategies we investigated for minimizing income tax were related to trying to lower our taxable income so that we would fall into a lower tax bracket.

2011 Tax Rates				
Taxable Income		$150,000		
Federal Tax Brackets	**Bracket Limit**	**Tax Rate**	**Incremental Tax Formula**	**Incremental Tax**
Up to $41,544	$41,544	15%	$41,544*0.15	$6,232
Between $41,545 and $83,088	$83,088	22%	($83,088-$41,544)*0.22	$9,140
Between $83,089 and $128,800	$128,800	26%	($128,000-$83,088)*0.26	$11,885
$128,801 and over	over $128,800	29%	($150,000-$128,000)*0.29	$6,148
Marginal Tax Rate	29%		Total Federal Tax	$33,404
Average Tax Rate ($31,825/$150,000)	21.22%		Less Personal Exemption	-$1,579
			Net Federal Tax	$31,825

Figure 21: Federal Tax Brackets and Tax Rates

Old Age Security and Age Amount Tax Credit

Old Age Security (OAS) provides a monthly government pension to seniors of at least age 65. In 2012, the maximum amount is set at approximately $545 per month, but you need at least 40 years residence in Canada and earn less than $69,562 in net income to receive the full amount. Not meeting these criteria would result in a reduction in the amount received. At some point, your income may exceed a maximum income level ($112,772 in 2012) beyond which you will not qualify for any OAS.

The age amount tax credit for seniors 65 or older is also subject to repayment for higher income levels. For 2012, the credit is $6,720 but clawback begins at net income of $33,884 and the benefit is eliminated at $78,864.

Both the payout and the net income repayment, or clawback, amounts for these benefits are indexed for inflation and rise each year to reflect increases in the cost of living.

When planning investment strategies to minimize tax impacts, it was important for us to try to find ways to stay as close to the OAS and/or age amount tax credit net income thresholds as possible in order to avoid triggering repayment obligations.

Canadian Dividends

Income generated from Canadian stock dividends results in lower taxes than employment, pension (RRSP, CPP, OAS) or interest income. This is because the company that distributed the dividend has already paid corporate tax on part of the profits from which the dividend was generated. To then tax the stockholder at full rates would become double taxation. This became an additional benefit of our retirement investment strategy (refer to the section "Retirement Investment Strategy"), which relied heavily on dividend income to fund our retirement spending. This meant that we required a lower gross income to generate our target yearly revenue.

The following oversimplified example shows the difference in federal income tax owing for $60,000 of income in Canadian dividends as opposed to other potential sources of retirement income, such as RRIF payments, CPP, OAS, interest from fixed income or dividends from non-Canadian stocks. While the other sources are taxed at the same rate as employment income, Canadian dividends are grossed up (by 141% in 2012) but then provide a generous dividend tax credit (0.164354 of the dividend income in 2012) that more than compensates in lowering the tax owing. We saw a similar pattern when calculating provincial tax (not shown in the example). The result was a much lower overall tax burden on the Canadian dividends when compared to other sources of income. (See Figure 22.)

Note that the gross-up may push income into a higher tax bracket where the excess income above the previous bracket is taxed at a higher marginal tax rate. The dividend tax credit is the same percentage regardless of tax bracket. This means the benefits of the tax credit decrease as the amount of dividend income increases. This is in line with the progressive tax strategy of taxing incrementally higher amounts of income at a higher rate.

	Canadian Dividends	Interest, RRIF, Foreign dividends
Income	$60,000.00	$60,000.00
Dividend Gross-up	$24,600.00	$0.00
Income after Dividend Gross-up	$84,600.00	$60,000.00
Marginal Tax Rate	26%	22%
Gross Federal Tax Owing	$15,764.12	$10,292.32
Basic Deductions	-$1,579.05	-$1,579.05
Dividend Tax Credit	-$13,904.35	
Net Federal Tax Owing	$280.72	$8,713.27

Figure 22: Tax on Canadian Dividends versus Other Income Sources

Because of the tax advantages of dividend income, we ensured that our non-registered investment account consisted totally of Canadian dividend-paying stocks since we paid tax annually on all income generated from this account. Any fixed income products (bonds, GICs) or non-Canadian stock would reside within our registered accounts, which are tax-sheltered until the money is withdrawn from them. At the point of withdrawal from a registered account, Canadian dividends would be taxed at the same rate as regular employment income and no extra tax advantage would be achieved.

Income Splitting

Canadian tax laws permit income splitting of retirement pensions and RRIFs between spouses starting at age 65. This means that even if one spouse will receive significantly higher retirement income from the various pension sources, he or she can allocate some of that revenue to the lower-earning spouse. The result of balancing income between spouses is a potentially lower tax bracket for the higher-earning spouse and therefore lower combined income taxes owed for the couple. Figure 23 demonstrates the potential savings realized by income splitting between spouses whose income levels differ greatly.

	Spouse #1	Spouse #2	Totals
No Income Split	$130,000.00	$20,000.00	$150,000.00
Gross Federal Tax	$27,568.12	$3,000.00	$30,568.12
Income Split	$75,000.00	$75,000.00	
Gross Federal Tax	$13,592.32	$13,592.32	$27,184.64
Tax Difference			$3,383.48

Figure 23: Income Splitting

Being able to reduce the income of the higher earner to fit into a lower tax bracket could amount to great savings. Unfortunately, the benefit of pension income splitting (including RRIFs) does not kick in until age 65 and does not apply to income from our non-registered account.

For early retirees like us, it was important to find other ways to balance our retirement incomes. The most obvious way was to open a spousal RRSP. This allows the higher-income spouse to make RRSP contributions and receive the tax deductions during the working years but have that money count as pension income for the lower-earning spouse in the retirement years. We used this vehicle to balance the values of our personal RRSPs.

After contributing the maximum allowable amounts to our RRSP and TFSA accounts, any extra savings would be invested in a non-registered investment account. To ensure income splitting in the retirement years, we made this a joint account and each declared half of the dividend income that was generated from it on our tax returns.

This effectively balanced our personal registered and non-registered sources of income. The only revenue source we could not effectively income split if we planned to withdraw from it before age 65 was our locked-in defined-contribution work RRSPs. There is no equivalent to a spousal RRSP to help in income splitting for Locked-in Retirement

Accounts (LIRAs). We would need to evaluate what tax implications the imbalance of Locked-in Retirement Income Fund (LRIF) income might cause when deciding when we should collapse our LIRAs into LRIFs.

Once we turn 65, we will be able to income split our CPP, RRIF and LIF payments if they are still divergent in size. We will evaluate whether doing so makes any difference to our combined marginal tax rate before bothering to proceed.

Models for Collapsing Investment Accounts

We thought about what was the best way to withdraw money from our various types of accounts (registered, non-registered, TFSA) in order to generate retirement income. We analyzed whether to use up the funds from our registered versus non-registered accounts first in order to fund our retirement. The usual advice from investment analysts and financial advisors in the past has been to use all of your non-registered funds first, then collapse the RRSPs at the end in order to maximize tax-free growth in those accounts. We questioned the soundness of this advice due to potential tax implications. To test our theories, we created models on a spreadsheet that played out the following scenarios:

1. Spend all the money in the non-registered account first, and then collapse the RRSPs and spend RRIF money one RRIF at a time
2. Collapse all the RRSPs up front and create RRIFs. Withdraw the annual minimum from each of the RRIF accounts and take the remaining funds required from the non-registered accounts at the same time

The results were very interesting and supported what we suspected. Following the traditional strategy of leaving the registered income to be used up last would allow it to grow and compound for many years tax-free. The problem is that we will be forced to collapse our RRSPs and turn them into RRIFs by age 71 and start withdrawing an annual minimum amount that starts at around 7.38% and rises each subsequent year. Since we will be taxed on the entire withdrawal at the regular income rate (as opposed to discounted dividend rates), a higher marginal tax rate and tax burden will result. Accordingly, we would need a higher gross income to achieve the same net spending income. This could also cause a reduction in our OAS entitlement if the amount of our RRIF withdrawal is higher than the OAS net income limit. The enforced minimum withdrawal would also be more than our dividends could cover, so we would be forced to sell stock at a rapid rate to generate enough cash, thus further lowering our dividend potentials. This would be a dangerous cycle that would deplete our registered accounts sooner than we planned.

In comparison, we looked at collapsing our RRSPs into RRIF accounts immediately upon retiring. We would source annual revenue by taking at least the minimum from the RRIFs plus the balance from our non-registered account. By doing so, we would deplete each type of account slower, giving them all more time to compound and grow, or at least not shrink. Each year, we would spread out the tax burden between RRIF income and dividend income from our non-registered account. This will result in a slight increase in our income tax in the early years but significantly reduce it in the later years compared to the first scenario. Overall in our lifespan, we will pay less tax and it seems our portfolio will last longer.

The following spreadsheet models support these findings. Not all the columns could be shown due to size, so some columns that did not show change in withdrawal patterns have been hidden. We picked the same artificial set of criteria for both scenarios. The criteria represent the total investments for a couple, but for simplicity, we show only one RRSP, TFSA and LIRA account for the couple as opposed to one per individual spouse.

- Total investment of $1.5 million made up of $415,000 RRSP, $40,000 TFSA, $150,000 LIRA and $900,000 in non-registered accounts.
- Inflation rate of 2%.
- Dividend yields of 4% for RRSP/LIRA/non-registered account. The TFSA was given a 6% yield to reflect our strategy of investing in riskier but higher-paying stocks in this account to maximize tax-free growth. For simplicity, assume any growth in stock value is offset by the rate of inflation.
- CPP of $700 × 2 per month for the couple, elected to start at age 65.
- OAS of $540 × 2 per month for the couple, starting at age 67.
- Gross income required for retirement spending plus taxes:
    - $66,000 when most of the revenue comes from dividends.
    - $72,000 when most of the revenue comes from RRIF; this amount was taken as an average to show more gross income is required for RRIF income than dividend income. It is not meant to represent the real tax implications for all years.

- Move \$5000 × 2 annually from the non-registered account to make TFSA contributions for the couple in order to shift more money into the tax-free account.
- Collapse the LIRA and convert it to a LIF at age 55, and proceed to withdraw the maximum allowable amount in order to free the locked up funds as quickly as possible.
- Initially withdraw only the dividends from the TFSA to supplement income, leaving the principal to grow tax-free for as long as possible.

In the first scenario, we will spend all the money from our non-registered account first, supplemented by the dividends of the TFSA. While we are withdrawing mainly from the non-registered account, the base gross amount needed is \$66,000 and is incremented by 2% annually for inflation. (See Figure 24.)

			Last Year of Work	Dividend Yield
Inflation	1.02			
CPP Amt per person	700	RRSP	410,000	1.04
OAS Amt per person	540	TFSA	40,000	1.06
TFSA Contribution for the couple	10,000	LIRA	150,000	1.04
Gross Income Dividends	66,000	Non Registered	900,000	1.04
Gross Income RRIF	72,000	Total	1,500,000	

Last Yr of Work	RRIF MIN - Formula to 71: 1/(90-age) then %	0.0244	0.0250	0.0286	0.0294	0.0400	0.0417	0.0435	0.0455	0.0476	0.0500	0.0526	0.0958	0.0993
	LIF MAX 2011 Ref Rate 6%			0.0651	0.0657	0.0738	0.0752	0.0767	0.0783	0.0802	0.0822	0.0845	0.1918	0.2240
48	Age at Jan 1 of Year	49	50	55	56	65	66	67	68	69	70	71	84	85
YR 0	Year	YR 1	YR2	YR 7	YR 8	YR 17	YR 18	YR 19	YR 20	YR 21	YR 22	YR 23	YR 36	YR 37
410,000	RRIF	426,400	443,456	539,532	561,113	798,639	830,585	863,808	898,360	924,235	897,649	868,465	182,490	114,665
	Withdraw Min	0	0	0	0	0	0	0	0	9,673	61,111	62,586	84,678	72,235
40,000	TFSA	49,856	60,277	115,260	126,139	199,440	145,067	99,573	49,983	0	0	0	0	0
	Withdrawl	2,400	2,991	5,602	6,260	23,533	62,583	51,131	52,419	49,983	0	0	0	0
150,000	LIRA	156,000	162,240	191,706	191,457	168,836	165,508	161,982	158,257	154,299	150,112	145,674	56,692	46,633
		0	0	12,593	11,086	12,691	12,696	12,694	12,683	12,692	12,683	12,684	12,693	12,699
900,000	Non Reg.	859,456	816,532	572,104	523,782	0	0	0	0	0	0	0	0	0
	Withdraw	73,600	74,329	66,131	68,467	37,579	0	0	0	0	0	0	0	0
	OAS			0	0	0	0	12,960	13,219	13,484	13,753	14,028	18,147	18,510
	CPP 65			0	0	16,800	17,136	17,479	17,828	18,185	18,549	18,920	24,474	24,964
	Spending Needs	66,000	67,320	74,327	75,813	90,604	92,416	94,264	96,150	98,073	100,034	102,035	131,993	134,633
	Spending All RRIF	70,000	71,400	78,831	80,408	96,095	98,017	99,977	101,977	104,016	106,097	108,219	139,992	142,792
1,500,000	Remaining At End of Year	1,491,712	1,482,505	1,418,601	1,402,492	1,166,915	1,141,160	1,125,363	1,106,600	1,078,534	1,047,761	1,014,139	239,182	161,298
	Total Withdrawals	76,000	77,320	84,327	85,813	90,604	92,416	94,264	96,150	104,016	106,097	108,219	139,992	128,408

Figure 24: Withdrawal Strategies – Use Up Non-registered Accounts First

Before the RRSP and LIRA are collapsed, they grow each year by the specified dividend yield percentages. The non-registered and TFSA accounts are reduced by the withdrawal amount first before the dividend yield growth rate is applied. The revenue stream is supplemented by LIF income at age 55, by CPP at age 65, and by OAS at age 67. The non-registered account runs out of money at age 65. At that point, we will start depleting the TFSA to continue to minimize taxes, while supplementing still with annual maximum withdrawals from the LIF. The TFSA money runs out at age 69, and then the tax issues start. The RRSP needs to be converted to a RRIF and will now bear the majority of the load for providing retirement income. Since we no longer have a dividend income or tax-free savings account to shield us, we will be taxed at a higher marginal tax rate. We reflect this in the example by now requiring the inflation prorated equivalent of $72,000 gross income instead of $67,000. By age 85, both the RRSP and the investment portfolio in general have run out of funds and can no longer cover future spending. In this scenario, we fall short of our planned end of retirement age of 90.

Note that even if the non-registered account or the TFSA had lasted longer, we would have been forced to collapse the RRSP at age 71 and start taking the minimum percentage, which would be 7.38% at that point. Since we had allowed the RRSP to grow so large by not withdrawing from it sooner, the minimum RRIF dollar withdrawal is fairly high by age 71. One way or another, for age 71 and beyond, the tax burden is heavy in this scenario.

			Last Year of Work	Dividend Yield
Inflation	1.02			
CPP Amt per person	700	RRSP	410,000	1.04
OAS Amt per person	540	TFSA	40,000	1.06
Gross Income (incl tax)	66,000	LIRA	160,000	1.04
TFSA Contr. For couple	10,000	Non Registered	900,000	1.04
		Total	1,500,000	

Last Yr of Work	RRIF MIN - Formula to 71: 1/(90-age) then %	0.0244	0.0250	0.0286	0.0294	0.0400	0.0417	0.0435	0.0833	0.0853	0.1133	0.1196	0.1271
	LIF MAX 2011 Ref Rate 6%			0.0651	0.0657	0.0738	0.0752	0.0767	0.1196	0.1281	0.5145	1.0000	1.0000
48	Age at Jan 1 of Year	49	50	55	56	65	66	67	79	80	88	89	90
YR 0	Year	YR 1	YR 2	YR 7	YR 8	YR 17	YR 18	YR 19	YR 31	YR 32	YR 40	YR 41	YR 42
410,000	RRIF	416,000	421,824	447,417	451,628	467,496	465,938	463,507	305,856	290,257	165,233	82,428	0
	Withdraw Min	10,000	10,400	12,653	13,159	18,730	19,479	20,258	27,425	26,762	23,318	85,975	82,428
40,000	TFSA	49,856	60,277	115,260	126,139	222,193	232,661	243,090	365,144	380,969	52,708	55,870	59,222
	Withdrawl	2,400	2,991	5,602	6,260	12,068	12,701	13,332	20,711	5,739	60,726	0	0
150,000	LIRA	156,000	162,240	191,706	191,457	168,836	165,508	161,982	99,039	91,534	12,698	0	0
		0	0	12,593	11,086	12,691	12,696	12,694	12,693	12,687	12,694	12,698	0
900,000	Non Reg.	869,856	838,164	664,219	633,268	308,819	279,152	261,675	37,377	0	0	0	0
	Withdraw	63,600	63,929	53,478	55,308	40,315	40,403	27,541	30,117	37,377	0	0	0
	OAS			0	0	0	0	12,960	16,436	16,765	19,643	20,036	20,437
	CPP 65			0	0	16,800	17,136	17,479	22,167	22,611	26,492	27,022	27,562
	Spending Needs	66,000	67,320	74,327	75,813	90,604	92,416	94,264	119,550	121,941	142,873	145,731	148,645
1,500,000	Remaining At End of Year	1,491,712	1,482,505	1,418,601	1,402,492	1,167,344	1,143,259	1,130,254	807,416	762,760	230,638	138,298	59,222
	Total Withdrawals	76,000	77,320	84,327	85,813	100,604	102,416	104,264	129,550	121,941	142,873	145,731	130,427

Figure 25: Withdrawal Strategies – Balanced – Use All Accounts at Once

In the second scenario where we immediately collapse the RRSP and start taking the minimum RRIF payment so that income is coming from the RRIF, TFSA and non-registered account at the same time, things look much better. The non-registered account lasts through age 79 and carries the lion's share of the revenue stream up until then. Since this account contains all dividend stock, the tax burden is lower throughout this period. Because the RRIF balance is reduced annually, the enforced minimum withdrawal amount remains relatively low. Once the non-registered account is depleted, the TFSA can carry the load tax-free until age 88. Only at age 89 will the RRIF bear major load, but there will be enough money to make it through that year. So we will make it to our predicted age 90 and can then rest in peace. (See Figure 25.)

The spreadsheet models clearly favoured the balanced approach of funding retirement income from all the accounts at once. But it was difficult to flaunt the conventional wisdom that had been drilled into us for so many years. We decided to verify our findings with experts and wrote to the Canadian personal financial magazine *MoneySense* to propose our theory.

MoneySense has several regular features that we thought could help us, including one called "Ask *MoneySense*" that answers questions sent in by their readers, as well as a column dedicated to retirement. All we hoped for from our communications with *MoneySense* was a reply to our email. Instead, we were contacted by David Ashton, one of the lead writers for the retirement column, who indicated that he wanted to write an article about our hypothesis. After several email and telephone exchanges where we provided information about our situation and clarified our questions, David consulted with various financial and retirement planning experts. We were very satisfied when these experts verified that what we had surmised was correct. The resultant article about it can be found here:
www.moneysense.ca/2011/10/27/how-to-tap-your-rrsp.

At the time of writing of that article, we were still aiming for our original goal of retirement at 55 and chose an arbitrarily large retirement sum as a guess of what we needed to live on. Only after we completed all of our research and calculations did we realize that we did not need as much money as we thought, and could retire earlier with a smaller sum, as long as we toned down our lifestyle expectations a bit. The reward of retiring seven years earlier made this more than worth it to us.

Tax-Free Savings Accounts versus RRSPs

We looked closely at the Tax-Free Savings Account (TFSA) when it first came out and concluded that it was one of the best savings incentives and tax shelters currently available. You are allowed to contribute up to $5000 per year per person regardless of income. While there are no immediate tax savings for the contribution, anything earned within a TFSA can subsequently be withdrawn tax-free. As a result, we found it advantageous to put the riskiest yet highest earning investment products from our preselected portfolio in these accounts. Since any increase in value in the TFSA is not taxed when it is earned or when money is withdrawn from the TFSA, we wanted to give it the best chance to grow and compound as quickly as possible.

We compared the TFSA to the RRSP to determine which would be more advantageous if you could afford to contribute to only one. We decided that for higher-income earners, the RRSP was more useful since it immediately lowered your taxable income and possibly kept you in a lower tax bracket. For us, whether or not we made a RRSP contribution often resulted in the difference between receiving a tax refund versus having to pay income tax.

For lower-income earners who were already in low tax brackets, the immediate benefits from the RRSP were significantly less and the possible negative impact on withdrawal were greater. Once the RRSP is turned into a RRIF, the income from it is taxed at the same rate as earned income. This could push low-income earners into a higher tax bracket that would then disqualify them from tax credits such as the Guaranteed Income Supplement, or may result in Old Age Security clawbacks. It would be much better for lower-income earners to contribute to the TFSA, which would result in tax-free income later on, without impacting their tax bracket.

Luckily this decision did not apply in our case, since we could afford to have the best of both worlds and maximize our contributions to both the TFSA and the RRSP. But it was still interesting to understand the differences. One other thing became clear: Even after we retired and could no longer contribute to the RRSP, we knew we should still try to contribute to the TFSA. Each year, we take money out of either our RRIF or non-registered account and use that to make the maximum TFSA contributions. In this way, we are slowly shifting our money from a taxable investment vehicle to a non-taxable one. We accounted for this strategy in our retirement budget.

RRSPs and RRIFs

We planned to fund our retirement income flow mainly from our non-registered account, but would need to supplement with some funds from our RRSPs. To accomplish this, we planned to convert them into Registered Retirement Income Funds (RRIF) once we stopped working and could no longer contribute to our RRSPs.

In our last working year, we would stay employed long enough to maximize our CPP contributions for that year and be entitled to each make one last RRSP contribution. We would contribute to the lower-valued RRSP and the spousal RRSP, continuing with our income-splitting goal (refer to the section "Income Splitting"). This meant we could not convert these RRSPs into RRIFs until the following year in order to leave them available to make the final contributions. This left the higher-valued RRSP that could be converted into a RRIF right away after our retirement and would start paying out income at the beginning of the next year.

Unlike the non-registered account where we could control the amount and timing of withdrawals, the RRIF has much stricter rules. Once a RRIF is created and income payments start flowing from it, there is a minimum amount that is required to be withdrawn every year. Up to and including age 70, the minimum is calculated with this formula:

1 ÷ (90 – Current age) × Value of RRIF on Dec 31 of the previous year

"Current age" refers to the age of the RRIF owner on January 1 of the calendar year when the income payments will begin. As the age grows, the percentage of withdrawal also gets larger. For people who want to keep their RRIF withdrawals as low as possible to avoid increasing taxable income, the age of the RRIF owner's younger spouse can be used if applicable. After age 70, the formula for withdrawal changes because it becomes a percentage specified by the government, so there is a big jump in percentage between age 70 and age 71. (See Figure 26.)

Age	% Withdrawal	Age	% Withdrawal	Age	% Withdrawal	Age	% Withdrawal	Age	% Withdrawal
48	2.38	53	2.70	58	3.13	63	3.70	68	4.55
49	2.44	54	2.78	59	3.23	64	3.85	69	4.76
50	2.50	55	2.86	60	3.33	65	4.00	70	5.00
51	2.56	56	2.94	61	3.45	66	4.17	71	7.3800
52	2.63	57	3.03	62	3.57	67	4.35	72	7.4800

Figure 26: RRIF Minimum Withdrawals by Year

A RRIF calculator to determine minimum withdrawal amounts can be found here: www.moneyville.ca/financialcalculators/retirement/858691.

To avoid paying more tax at the full income rate, we wanted to minimize the amount we withdrew from our RRIFs each year. We did this by specifying the age of the younger spouse to be used for the withdrawal formula and by requesting that the minimum amount be withdrawn.

By withdrawing only the minimum from our RRIF each year, we also avoid paying withholding tax (immediate taxation of funds at the point of payment). This effectively deferred income tax on RRIF income for up to another year.

This was all handled by our online investment broker, Scotia iTRADE. It took about a week to open the RRIF account and then six weeks for the transfer of funds from RRSP to RRIF to fully take effect. For several months afterwards, residual dividends continued to be paid to the RRSP instead of the RRIF. We repeatedly needed to call Scotia iTRADE to transfer these sums over until the stocks finally recognized the RRIF as their new home.

Our target dividend yield of 4% would cover the rising minimum percentage that we needed to withdraw from our RRIF each year until around age 65. So for that duration, we could continue to follow our retirement strategy of living on the dividends while preserving the capital. After age 65, the minimum percentages would start to exceed the amount we hoped to generate from dividends. At that point, we would have to sell some of the capital to generate enough cash in the minimum. This is not so bad, since by then we would probably need more money to account for inflation anyway.

If we can afford to, we will probably wait until the end of a calendar year to sell stock and make the RRIF withdrawal. Since we are allowed to withdraw from the RRIF any time within the calendar year, choosing to wait until the end of the year allows the money to grow tax-free for one more year.

If it turns out we do not need the RRIF withdrawal to spend, we can consider making the RRIF withdrawal in kind. This means we can withdraw investments (stocks or bonds) from the RRIF and transfer it to either our TFSA (pending contribution room) or our non-registered account. This will preserve the capital and dividends from these investments and merely shift them to a different account.

LIRAs and LIFs

Our locked-in defined contribution work RRSPs were converted into self-directed Locked-in Retirement Accounts (LIRAs) once we left our jobs. They act as tax shelters just like RRSPs, except there are even more restrictions on them. Our money accumulated in the LIRA cannot be accessed until at least age 55. At that point, it can be converted into a Life Income Fund (LIF), which is like a RRIF with more strings attached. The LIF has the same yearly minimum withdrawal conditions as the RRIF, but it also imposes a yearly maximum. The aim is to ensure the money in the LIF lasts our lifetime. The maximum allowable withdrawal is the greater of the RIF's investment earnings from last year (including interest, dividends and capital gains) or a maximum withdrawal percentage depending on age.

The maximum withdrawal percentages are updated yearly and published at the end of the year for the following year. Figure 27 shows the 2012 maximums for Ontario. They are documented in the "2012 Life Income Fund (LIF) and Locked-in Retirement Income Fund (LRIF) Maximum Annual Income Payment Amount Table," index number L200-411. This can be found on the Financial Services Commission of Ontario website: www.fsco.gov.on.ca/en/pensions/policies/active/Documents/L200-411.pdf.

LIF Maximum Withdrawal for 2012

Age on Jan 1st	Max %	Age on Jan 1st	Max %	Age on Jan 1st	Max %	Age on Jan 1st	Max %	Age on Jan 1st	Max %
55	6.50697	62	7.03703	69	8.01930	76	10.14952	83	16.89953
56	6.56689	63	7.14124	70	8.22496	77	10.65661	84	19.18515
57	6.62952	64	7.25513	71	8.45480	78	11.25255	85	22.39589
58	6.69833	65	7.37988	72	8.71288	79	11.96160	86	27.22561
59	6.77285	66	7.51689	73	9.00423	80	12.81773	87	35.32938
60	6.85367	67	7.66778	74	9.33511	81	13.87002	88	51.45631
61	6.94147	68	7.83449	75	9.71347	82	15.19207	89	100.00000

Figure 27: 2012 Ontario LIF Maximum Percentages

Payments from the LIFs will be taxed at the same income tax rates as the RRIFs. But whereas our strategy was to take out as little as possible (the minimum) from the RRIFs per year, our goal for the LIF was to take out the maximum allowable. Since we are limited to how much we can withdraw, we wanted to take every opportunity to remove as much as we could from this restrictive fund so that the balance of its value will not outlast our lifetimes. Because we planned to take out more than the minimum amount, there will be a withholding tax that will range from 10% for amounts of $5000 or less up to 30% for amounts exceeding $15,000.

Because of the new Ontario LIF rules that came into effect January 1, 2011, when we convert our LIRAs into LIFs, we have a one-time opportunity to withdraw up to 50% of the LIF's value. We must submit a form requesting to do this within 60 days of creating the new LIF. This would free half of our LIF value from the restrictive maximums, giving us better control over our money. Each of us plans to transfer this LIF money into our RRIF, so there should be no tax implications to this transaction.

There is also an option for applying to unlock the funds from LIF accounts if the total value of the funds in all of your locked-in accounts is less than a given total that changes each year. In 2012, this amount was $20,040. One of us has very little money in our LIF and might actually qualify for this case after having applied to transfer 50% of its value to our RRIF. We will keep this in mind when the time comes to see if the option is still available.

Canada Pension Plan

The Canada Pension Plan provides a monthly pension plan to seniors who have made contributions to the plan while employed. The most common age to start taking it is at 65, but you can begin as early as age 60 or defer it up to age 70. There is a significant penalty for starting CPP payments prior to 65 and a large reward for waiting until 70. In the past, the penalty or reward was set at 0.5% per month, or a 30% difference if taking CPP at 60 or 70 instead of 65. Recent changes have been implemented to encourage people to take CPP later as opposed to earlier. This is done by increasing both the reward for waiting up to age 70 and the penalty for taking CPP as early as age 60. The penalty per month for taking CPP earlier than age 65 is gradually increasing from 0.5% and will reach 0.6% by 2016. The reward each month that you wait after age 65 before taking CPP will rise from 0.5% to 0.7% by 2013. (See Figure 28.) As of 2012, you do not need to be retired to start taking CPP.

Description	2010	2011	2012	2013	2014	2015	2016
% Low Income Years Dropped	15.0%	15.0%	16.0%	17.0%	17.0%	17.0%	17.0%
Monthly Reduction for Early CPP Before 65	0.50	0.50	0.52	0.54	0.56	0.58	0.60
Reduction for Taking CPP at 60	30.0%	30.0%	31.2%	32.4%	33.6%	34.8%	36.0%
Monthly Increment for Late CPP after 65	0.50	0.57	0.64	0.70	0.70	0.70	0.70
Increase for Taking CPP at 70	30.0%	32.7%	38.4%	42.0%	42.0%	42.0%	42.0%

Figure 28: Canada Pension Plan Changes from 2011 through 2016

The changes in percentages are gradually being introduced so that by 2013, you will get 0.7% extra for each month you wait to take CPP, up to 42% if you wait until age 70. By 2016, you will be penalized 0.6% per month for taking CPP earlier than age 65, up to 36% for starting at 60.

The CPP payout that you qualify to receive is calculated based on the amount of contributions that you made during the eligible contribution period, starting from age 18 up to the age that you start taking CPP. If you take CPP at 65, the period comes to 47 years (65 – 18). At age 60, that period reduces to 42 years, and at 70, it rises to 52 years. Everyone is allowed to drop a given percentage (15% as of 2011) of their lowest income years. The 47 years of eligible contributions at age 65 would allow 7 years to be dropped ($47 \times 0.15 = 7.05$), so only your best 40 years are counted. At age 60, 6 years would be dropped ($42 \times 0.15 = 6.3$), so your best 36 years are counted. This dropout percentage is rising to 16% in 2012 and by 2014, the value will be at 17%, allowing for eight years of low income to be dropped. There are extra conditions for dropping low-income years, including child-rearing years, and periods when you are entitled to disability pension.

To get the maximum CPP payout, you would have to earn enough pensionable income during the years that are counted so that each year results in maximum CPP contribution. For any year that the maximum contribution was not made, you get only partial credit and your CPP payout is reduced accordingly. If your contribution was below a minimum, you will not even get partial credit and this will be considered a zero-contribution year.

The implications of early retirement weighed heavily on the complex formula for determining our CPP payouts and affected our decision about what age we should start taking it. Retiring at age 48 means we will have 17 extra zero-income and zero-contribution years to deal with if we take the payout at age 65. Even after being allowed to drop seven or eight low-income years, we still have many left to contend with. Taking CPP early at age 60 would reduce our base amount, but it would also eliminate five of the zero-contribution years from our total. We needed to analyze the final impact of these two opposing factors.

The first step in understanding our potential Canada Pension Plan payouts was to sign up for a Service Canada account that provides online information about various government programs such as CPP, OAS and unemployment insurance. You can register for this account at the Service Canada website (www.servicecanada.gc.ca/eng/online/mysca.shtml). (See Figure 29.) After filling in the registration form, it takes multiple weeks for it to be processed and then you are sent a seven-digit Personal Access Code by mail. You need to enter this code only the first time you log in to your account. Thereafter, you can log in using the user ID and password that you set up during registration.

Figure 29: Service Canada Account Registration

From this account, you can see the history of your annual pensionable earnings and CPP contributions relative to the yearly maximums and minimums. Based on this information, it provides an estimate of what your CPP payout would be if you were 65 today, what it would be reduced to if you started payments at age 60, and what it would increase to at age 70. (See Figure 30.) These figures are only useful as you get closer to the relevant ages. It does not help much for early retirement planning purposes.

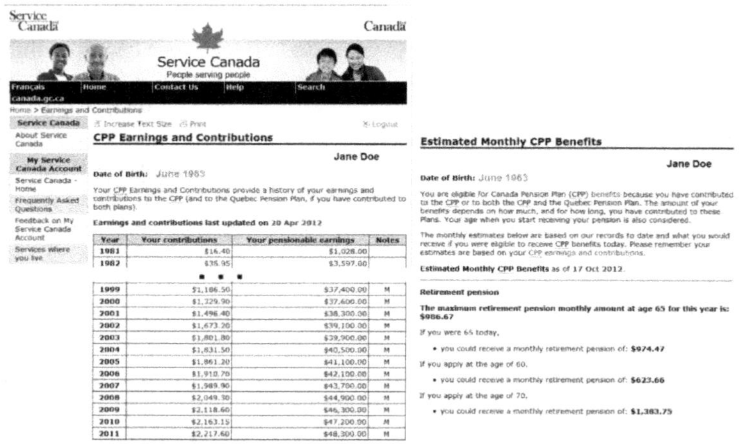

Service Canada

Canada

Service Canada
People serving people

Français | Home | Contact Us | Help | Search
canada.gc.ca

Home > Earnings and Contributions

Service Canada
About Service Canada

My Service Canada Account
Service Canada - Home
Frequently Asked Questions
Feedback on My Service Canada Account
Services where you live

Increase Text Size | Print | Logout

CPP Earnings and Contributions

Jane Doe

Date of Birth: June 1963

Your CPP Earnings and Contributions provide a history of your earnings and contributions to the CPP (and to the Quebec Pension Plan, if you have contributed to both plans).

Earnings and contributions last updated on 20 Apr 2012

Year	Your contributions	Your pensionable earnings	Notes
1981	$16.40	$1,028.00	
1982	$35.95	$3,597.00	

■ ■ ■

Year	Your contributions	Your pensionable earnings	Notes
1999	$1,186.50	$37,400.00	M
2000	$1,329.90	$37,600.00	M
2001	$1,496.40	$38,300.00	M
2002	$1,673.20	$39,100.00	M
2003	$1,801.80	$39,900.00	M
2004	$1,831.50	$40,500.00	M
2005	$1,861.20	$41,100.00	M
2006	$1,910.70	$42,100.00	M
2007	$1,989.90	$43,700.00	M
2008	$2,049.30	$44,900.00	M
2009	$2,118.60	$46,300.00	M
2010	$2,163.15	$47,200.00	M
2011	$2,217.60	$48,300.00	M

Estimated Monthly CPP Benefits

Jane Doe

Date of Birth: June 1963

You are eligible for Canada Pension Plan (CPP) benefits because you have contributed to the CPP or to both the CPP and the Quebec Pension Plan. The amount of your benefits depends on how much, and for how long, you have contributed to these Plans. Your age when you start receiving your pension is also considered.

The monthly estimates below are based on our records to date and what you would receive if you were eligible to receive CPP benefits today. Please remember your estimates are based on your CPP earnings and contributions.

Estimated Monthly CPP Benefits as of 17 Oct 2012.

Retirement pension

The maximum retirement pension monthly amount at age 65 for this year is: $986.67

If you were 65 today,

- you could receive a monthly retirement pension of: **$974.47**

If you apply at the age of 60,

- you could receive a monthly retirement pension of: **$623.66**

If you apply at the age of 70,

- you could receive a monthly retirement pension of: **$1,383.75**

Figure 30: Service Canada Account – CPP Contributions and Payment Estimates

There is an option to run through a "Canadian Retirement Income Calculator" that allows you to change some of the basic parameters for the payout estimation. (See Figure 31.) One of the variables that the calculator allows you to modify is the anticipated future earnings between the current age and the age when CPP payments are to start. A dropdown menu allows you to pick $0 as the amount of income, which seems perfect for estimating early retirement with no income from the retirement age through to age 65. Unfortunately there is an error in the calculator when $0 is selected as the income. The results provided are the same as if the maximum income was earned, which cannot be correct. The results are a bit better, although still not correct when $5000 is chosen as the income, and as expected, the payout is reduced significantly.

The way to get the best payout estimate when retiring early and taking CPP at ages 65 or 60 or 70 is to call the Service Canada help line (1-800-277-9914) and ask the operator to perform the calculations for you. If you provide your last date of work, the operator can run simulations for taking CPP at the various ages. The example in Figure 32 shows how early retirement impacts the projected payout values and reviews some factors in the decision of when to start taking CPP. All figures are rounded to the nearest dollar.

The CPP maximum payout for 2012 is $987. Assume that based on your Service Canada employment profile, the CPP payout estimate if you are age 65 today is around $975, reduced to $624 if you took it at age 60, and increases to $1384 if you wait until age 70. Using the Service Canada retirement calculator and indicating that your future yearly earnings from age 48 through 65 is zero produces the exact same estimates. This is obviously wrong, since there is a definite penalty for having no pensionable income and not contributing to CPP from ages 48 to 65. Changing the future yearly earnings to the next lowest amount, which is $5000, produces more-reasonable results. The estimate for age 65 reduces from $974 to $774, while age 60 reduces from $624 to $541. As expected, the extra zero CPP contribution years caused by early retirement results in a reduction of payout across the board regardless of what age you take it at.

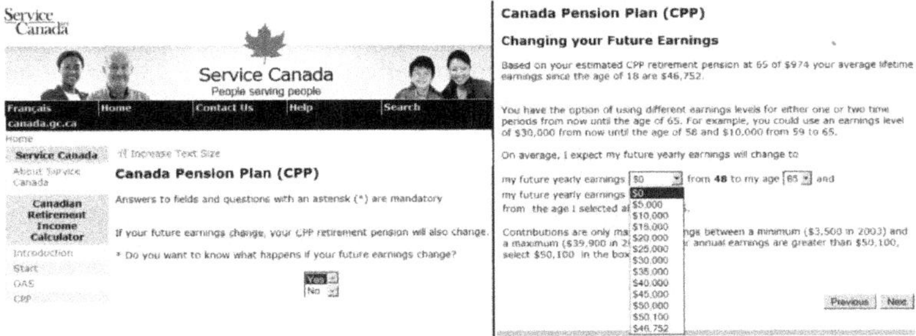

Figure 31: Service Canada Account – Canadian Retirement Income Calculator

Calling Service Canada and asking for a simulation produces similar results to the ones produced by the calculator with $5000 future earnings, but the impact of early retirement is even more severe. By ceasing to work at age 48, the projected payout at age 65 falls to $681. Taking it at age 60 further reduces the payout to $488. Note that in the early retirement scenario, the impact of taking CPP early at age 60 is partially balanced by having five fewer eligible years of zero income (between 60 and 65). For the initial estimate, if we were 65 today, taking CPP early at age 60 would have reduced the payment by 36% (1 – (624 ÷ 974)). By retiring at age 48, the impact of taking CPP at age 60 reduces the payment by only 28% (1 – (488 ÷ 681)). So after we analyzed the impact of early retirement on the CPP payouts, the question remained: At what age should we start taking it?

Max: $987	Take CPP Payout at Age:				
Estimate Source	**60**	**65**	**70**	**% Decrease 65->60**	**% Increase 65-> 70**
If you were 65 today	$624	$974	$1,384	36%	30%
~~Retirement Calculator - $0 income from age 48~~	~~$624~~	~~$974~~	~~$1,384~~	~~36%~~	~~30%~~
Retirement Calculator - $5000 income from age 48	$541	$774	$987	30%	22%
Simulation by Service Canada Operator for retiring at age 48	$488	$681	$967	28%	30%
Payment Reduction because of early retirement	22%	30%	30%		

Figure 32: CPP Payout Estimates

Is having five years of extra CPP payments worth the reduced rate received? Will waiting five extra years be worth the larger monthly amounts that will be paid? Part of the answer is determined by life expectancy. Will we live long enough to make waiting worthwhile? Another factor relates to how much we really needed the extra money earlier in order to meet day-to-day expenses. Also there's the consideration of which years we can make best use of the extra money. At 60, we might be able to use the funds to travel more while we are still healthy, while by 70 we may start to slow down too much to fully enjoy it.

Comparing the examples of taking CPP at age 60 versus age 65, it would take until age 79 for the CPP payment taken at age 65 to catch up and eventually exceed the CPP payments starting from age 60. The calculations assume a 2% index for inflation. (See Figure 33.) Since our retirement predictions all assumed that we would live to age 90, it will be better in the long run for us to wait to start CPP until age 65. If by age 60, we find that we are short of funds to cover our expenses, we still have the option to change our minds and start earlier. But during our planning, it seemed a better bet to have larger CPP payments in our later years as a continued hedge against inflation.

	60	61	62	63	64	65	66	67	68	69	70	71	72	73	74	75	76	77	78	79	SUM
CPP Age 60	488	498	508	518	528	539	550	561	572	583	595	607	619	631	644	657	670	683	697	711	$11,857
CPP Age 65	0	0	0	0	0	681	695	709	723	737	752	767	782	798	814	830	847	864	881	899	$11,777
Assume 2% Inflation																				Diff	80

Figure 33: CPP Payouts – Age 60 versus 65

Generating Income Flow to Pay Monthly Expenses

Since we already had a working model for paying monthly bills with little fuss and intervention, there was no need for much change after retirement. Most of our expenses continue to be automatically deducted out of our chequing account by pre-authorized payment agreements, or automatically charged to our credit card. Once a month we continue to manually pay the full amount of our credit card bill. The main difference now is how we keep this chequing account with sufficient cash flow to cover the monthly expenses.

Now retired, we no longer have our regular salary deposits flowing into our bank chequing account in order to cover our monthly expenses. Instead we are relying on our RRIF payments, dividends from our non-registered account, and eventually, LIRA, OAS and CPP payments. The RRIF, LIRA, OAS and CPP pension payments can be arranged to be direct deposited into the chequing account.

We plan to monitor the dividends that are paid into the non-registered account and manually transfer them over to the chequing account regularly. This is partly because a monthly automatic transfer would be complicated since we have so many different stocks that pay out different amounts at different frequencies and dates. More important, we need to continue to keep an eye on our dividend payouts to ensure there is no significant cut in yield for any particular stock.

Dividends from the stock we own are paid out either monthly or quarterly. This means that we can expect the same dividend payout on a three-month cycle. For example, January, April, July and October will pay out the same dividend amounts (unless there is a pre-declared change in dividend yield) on the same date range (within one or two business days). We have noticed that our discount broker Scotia iTRADE needs a one-business-day delay to update our portfolio with new dividend payouts. If our dividend is due on the 15th of the month, we will usually see it on the 16th. However, if the dividend is paid out on a Friday or over the weekend, we often do not see the dividends in our account until the following Tuesday, since they need Monday to process it. The delay may even stretch to Wednesday if Monday is a holiday. Once we receive the dividends, then it takes one or two business days to transfer that money to our bank account where it can be used to pay the bills.

The bottom line is that we cannot be dependent on the new dividends to arrive in time to cover our upcoming expenses. Therefore, we have the need for a cash float to be the true source of our income. Any new dividends will be added to the cash float once they become available. We set up a high-interest savings account to act as the float. This savings account is in the same bank as our chequing account for ease of money transfer between them. We initially stocked the float up with enough money to cover three months of expenses, plus an extra lump sum to cover emergencies. We have scheduled automatic transfers from the savings account to the chequing account at the beginning of each month for a fixed amount representing our anticipated monthly spending needs. Throughout the month, we monitor our credit card bill and other expenses so that we can anticipate if there is an unusual spending spike that might require a top-up to the regular transfer from the float. If so, an extra manual transfer is created to ensure the chequing account can cover all the bills.

To keep track of the various dates that we need to move money around from our Scotia iTRADE investment accounts to our bank savings or chequing accounts, we keep an online calendar. We created repeating reminder tasks that fall on the same day of each month, and the calendar sends a reminder email on any day where there is a task to complete.

High-Interest Savings Accounts

Since we plan to keep a fairly large cash float for emergencies, we want to be able to earn a relatively good interest rate on it. It is useful to be able to monitor relative interest rates that financial institutions are offering for savings and chequing accounts on a regular basis.

For example, some savings accounts pay as little as 0.3% or less annually, while others may pay 1.35% or more. If we were to keep a $25,000 cash float, the difference in yearly interest payments would be $75 or less as opposed to $320 or more. It pays to choose wisely when picking a savings account.

We found the website for Cannex Financial Exchanges (www.cannex.com), which provides interest rates and product information for financial products across Canada on a daily basis. (See Figure 34.) Some parts of this website are subscription-based, but the report on deposit accounts is free.

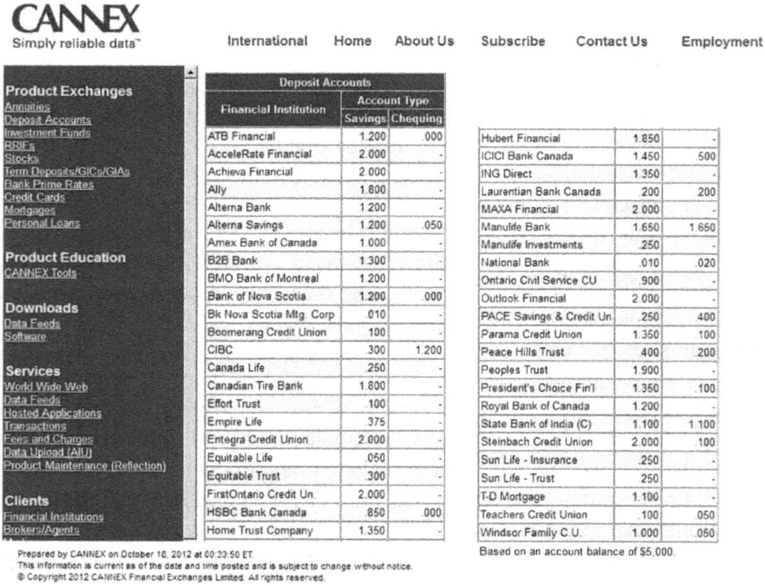

CANNEX
Simply reliable data™

International Home About Us Subscribe Contact Us Employment

Product Exchanges
Annuities
Deposit Accounts
Investment Funds
RRIFs
Stocks
Term Deposits/GICs/GIAs
Bank Prime Rates
Credit Cards
Mortgages
Personal Loans

Product Education
CANNEX Tools

Downloads
Data Feeds
Software

Services
World Wide Web
Data Feeds
Hosted Applications
Transactions
Fees and Charges
Data Upload (AIU)
Product Maintenance (Reflection)

Clients
Financial Institutions
Brokers/Agents

Deposit Accounts		
Financial Institution	Account Type	
	Savings	Chequing
ATB Financial	1.200	.000
AcceleRate Financial	2.000	-
Achieva Financial	2.000	-
Ally	1.800	-
Alterna Bank	1.200	-
Alterna Savings	1.200	.050
Amex Bank of Canada	1.000	-
B2B Bank	1.300	-
BMO Bank of Montreal	1.200	-
Bank of Nova Scotia	1.200	.000
Bk Nova Scotia Mtg. Corp	.010	-
Boomerang Credit Union	.100	-
CIBC	.300	1.200
Canada Life	.250	-
Canadian Tire Bank	1.800	-
Effort Trust	.100	-
Empire Life	.375	-
Entegra Credit Union	2.000	-
Equitable Life	.050	-
Equitable Trust	.300	-
FirstOntario Credit Un.	2.000	-
HSBC Bank Canada	.850	.000
Home Trust Company	1.350	-
Hubert Financial	1.850	-
ICICI Bank Canada	1.450	.500
ING Direct	1.350	-
Laurentian Bank Canada	.200	.200
MAXA Financial	2.000	-
Manulife Bank	1.650	1.650
Manulife Investments	.250	-
National Bank	.010	.020
Ontario Civil Service CU	.900	-
Outlook Financial	2.000	-
PACE Savings & Credit Un	.250	.400
Parama Credit Union	1.350	.100
Peace Hills Trust	.400	.200
Peoples Trust	1.900	-
President's Choice Fin'l	1.350	.100
Royal Bank of Canada	1.200	-
State Bank of India (C)	1.100	1.100
Steinbach Credit Union	2.000	.100
Sun Life - Insurance	.250	-
Sun Life - Trust	.250	-
T-D Mortgage	1.100	-
Teachers Credit Union	.100	.050
Windsor Family C.U.	1.000	.050

Based on an account balance of $5,000.

Prepared by CANNEX on October 18, 2012 at 00:33:50 ET.
This information is current as of the date and time posted and is subject to change without notice.
© Copyright 2012 CANNEX Financial Exchanges Limited. All rights reserved.

Figure 34: Cannex Deposit Accounts – Sample of Interest Rates Calculated Daily

Saving for Larger Capital Expenditures after Retirement

Once we retired and started getting monthly income flow primarily from our dividends and RRIF payments, it became more difficult to save for larger expenditures. We probably will need a new car in about four or five years, and we debated how to fund this. We could sell some stock at the time we need the car to get a big block of money at once.

But doing so will reduce our abilities to generate dividends and might also incur capital gain costs. Another strategy would be to slowly save for the purchase by siphoning off a portion of our dividends each month. We actually accounted for this in our monthly budget, but now it was time to execute on the plan. We decided to open up another savings account separate from our cash float for capital expenditure savings, so that it was clear how much we had for this purpose as opposed to the regular cash flow for paying bills. We looked into creating an account with one of the more obscure financial institutions that were paying the highest interest rates. We researched to make sure that they were secure and that money could be easily transferred between these types of accounts and our regular savings account. If the capital expenditure becomes an emergency before we are able to save enough money, then we can always borrow from the cash float or still go back to the original idea of selling stock. But at least we leave those options as the last resort while we try to slowly save for our big-ticket items.

Final Retirement Preparations

In our final push towards early retirement, we needed to complete some final preparations, including maximizing potential benefits at work and getting all imminent big expenditures out of the way.

Maximizing Final Work Benefits

We wanted to expense as many medical, dental and vision costs as possible while we were still covered by our work medical benefits. We scheduled appointments with our optometrists and finally ordered those prescription reading glasses that we've been putting off for years. We checked in with our dentists to see if there were any pressing issues with our teeth that needed to be addressed. We refilled any drug prescriptions on the company's dime for the last time. I got a prescription from my doctor for a TENS electrical nerve stimulation machine to relieve chronic muscle pain and was able to expense that before retiring. I used up the last of my flexible health care expense account on final massages that would become an extraneous luxury after retirement.

Get Imminent Big Capital Expenditures Out of the Way

We knew that once we moved into the retirement phase, it would take longer to save up for larger planned expenditures such as longer vacations, a new car, new appliances or other home repairs, or any extravagant splurges. While we did set aside a cash float for emergencies, we did not want to tap into that right away for expensive outlays that we could anticipate coming up in the near future. We wanted to continue working until we had the savings to take care of them. Where we could, we either made the new purchase or performed the repair ahead of time. Otherwise, we set aside enough extra money on top of our regular cash float in anticipation of the upcoming expenses before deciding we had earned enough to stop working.

What to Do With All This Free Time?

When we told people that we were planning on early retirement, we were surprised by how many times we were asked, "What will you do with all that free time? Won't you be bored?" Others have stated something to the effect of, "I'm not ready yet for retirement. I still want the mental stimulation and challenges that work brings me."

These considerations have never occurred to us. We both have such a wide range of interests and hobbies that we could rattle off ideas of things to do ad infinitum. Our issue has always been not having enough time to pursue them. And we have many ways to challenge and mentally stimulate ourselves while having fun as opposed to being stressed out at work. Since retiring, we've actually found ourselves busier than ever, with still not enough time to do all the things on our wish list. Having more time has opened up so many new opportunities that now fill our days.

It is obvious from the questions we received and stories that we've been told about other retirees that it is as important to prepare mentally and emotionally for retirement as it is to be ready financially. Retirement could mean a big change in lifestyle, and change can be scary. We've heard about people who cannot adapt to the slower pace (what slower pace, we ask?) and wither away to ill health through isolation or inactivity, or retirees who seem to spend their days wandering aimlessly in the shopping malls. If this is their idea of retired life, then we can understand how this would not appeal.

But with a little bit of forethought, investigation and planning, a whole new world of freedom and adventure can be available for the taking. Even with all our many ideas of what we might do in our retirement, we benefited from some preparation and structure to turn our concepts into reality. So what did we plan to do with all our new free time?

Travel has always been a passion of ours, so we made our bucket list of all the exotic locations that we would like to visit in our lifetimes. We picked a few that we would like to tackle in the near future and did research on what they had to offer. We looked more seriously at different home-swap websites to determine if they were worth signing up for. We have made plans for road trips and day trips closer to home, incorporating themes like a cycling trip, a drive to see autumn leaves, or to see a play or two in some little town. We want to take more cruises, including a Baltic cruise and river cruises through Europe.

We investigated ways of learning new skills or improving on existing ones that appealed to us. This ranged from self-study to taking lessons or adult learning classes. Some of our areas of interest include learning conversational French, writing Chinese, regional cooking, how to take good black and white photographs, crocheting, playing the ukulele, art history, creative writing, improving our tennis game and much more.

We looked into the website called Meetup (www.meetup.com) that connects you with other people who share a common interest in some topic. For example, you could meet with other film enthusiasts to talk about classic movies or to view a new film and discuss it afterwards. There are also groups that get together to play sports, go hiking, knit, play board games, try out restaurants together — the list goes on and on.

We made note of the dates and times of local festivals, walking tours, farmers' markets, talks, concerts, exhibitions, shows and other events that we could attend. There are so many opportunities that interest us that we need an online calendar to keep track of them.

We pledged to eat better, do some sort of exercise daily, lose weight and live a healthier lifestyle. This was all easier to follow through on once we had the time and could actually implement and follow a routine.

We were able to allocate more time to spend with our elderly parents and to see friends and family more often. We actually had time to go out for lunch or an after-work drink with our old work colleagues. There was rarely time for lunch while we were still working!

We researched opportunities to volunteer at causes that interested us. This would give us the opportunity to interact with others and give back a bit to our community.

We planned to continue to do all the activities we enjoyed and participated in before retirement, but we could do more of it. This included dining out, going to live theatre, working out at the gym, playing tennis, cycling, going to art galleries and museums, going for long walks, cooking and giving dinner parties, reading, writing and blogging, watching movies, knitting, photography — we had no shortage of interests or hobbies.

We love entertaining and getting together with our friends. We belong to a book club where each member is given an opportunity to host the event and select the book to be read. This results in an eclectic reading list that pushes us out of our comfort zone and into exploring different book genres that we might not have tried on our own. The book club is also a great excuse to see each other, gossip and have a great meal. We belong to a dinner club with two other couples where each dinner is a themed event. The host couple picks a country and prepares the main course, while the others bring the appetizer and dessert. We like playing board games and card games and have hosted and attended games nights, as well as frequenting the games cafe Snakes & Lattes in Toronto.

Now that we've retired, I am hoping that retirement will allow me more time to write about our experiences in the three blogs that I maintain — a travel blog, a dining blog and one about our experiences around town. Ironically, we are so busy now with all the travelling and extra activities that so far there has been less than to blog and more things to blog about.

We've even created a "honey-do" list of all the non-urgent chores or renovations that we've wanted to do around our home but never made their way to the top of our priority rankings while we were busy working. It's funny that we still haven't found time for many of these items yet as we bask in the early glow of freedom from the rat race. For now, we are too busy playing.

To us, adjusting to retirement came easily because these were all things that we enjoyed and wanted to do. This is why we wanted to retire early in the first place. So far, it hasn't really sunk in that we are retired for good. It feels like we are on a long, extended vacation and still have to cram in all our moments of enjoyment before this all comes to an end. Eventually we should learn to slow down ... or maybe not. Perhaps it is our lot in life to work hard and play hard. But playing hard is so much more fun.

For those who don't find "playing" to be natural, it is important to plan ahead and develop some hobbies and interests. Retirement life is so much more enjoyable and fulfilling when you have things to look forward to and a reason to get up in the mornings.

The Later Years

There is a lot of information and support for the typical retirement years starting at 65, or 60, or even 55, which is usually the benchmark for early retirement. At age 48, we were "on the road less travelled by" to paraphrase the famous Robert Frost poem *The Road Not Taken.* Accordingly, we concentrated much of our planning and investigation on how we would survive these early retirement years.

To have a full retirement plan, we also needed to put some thought into what would happen in the later years. The processes of monitoring and administering our own finances and investments to ensure sufficient money flow to pay our bills requires that we stay in sharp mental and physical conditions. As we age, at some point all this will become too onerous for us to continue to handle on our own. We have thought through what we plan to do at that point.

Annuities

Annuities can be used as a self-funded pension that will pay out a regular sum of money for some specified period of time, up to the duration of your lifetime. Annuities cost more and pay out less at younger ages since they will need to pay for more years. Payouts are also affected by the current interest rates at the time of the purchase, so buying an annuity when interest rates are low will lock you into a lower payment even after interest rates start to rise. For these reasons, we would not consider an annuity until much later in our retirement.

We may get to a stage where we would choose to cash in some or all of our investments to buy an annuity that would pay out enough to meet our spending needs. This assumes that we would have enough funds left to do this, or we could sell our home and use that capital to purchase the annuity. The annuity would take care of providing the monthly cash flow and alleviate the need for us to manipulate our investment portfolio for this purpose.

Annuities can pay out for a fixed duration, or for the lifetime of either the purchaser or both the purchaser and his or her spouse. It also may or may not be indexed for inflation. You can select a number of guaranteed years that the annuity will pay out even if you die prior to that span of time. Obviously, the more features added, the higher the price of the annuity or the lower the payouts. A joint (paid as long as either spouse is alive), lifetime, inflation-indexed annuity with a longer guaranteed payment period costs the most, and the price increases the younger you are when you buy the annuity.

It seemed important to carefully evaluate each extra feature to assess whether it was worth the price, and how long we would have to live before we recouped enough payments to see the benefits. For example, since we do not have any children or dependents, it did not seem worthwhile to pay extra for a guaranteed period of payments after our deaths. Looking at inflation-indexed annuities, we discovered that they were rare and difficult to find in Canada. This was another feature where we questioned whether it was worth the price to get a significantly lower payout for the same premium investment. Perhaps it was better to let the OAS and CPP pensions handle the inflation component and settle for a higher annuity payment.

Looking at annuity pricing charts for 2012, for $100,000 in premiums, Figure 35 shows examples of the monthly payouts at various ages for a joint, non-indexed, no-guarantee life annuity from various providers. The companies we sampled included BMO Insurance, Canada Life, Desjardins Financial Security, Empire Life, Standard Life and Sun Life Assurance Company. All the providers pay a higher monthly sum as the age rises. It was interesting to note that different companies charged relatively more or less than the others at different ages.

Joint Annuity	55	60	65	69	70	75	80
High	378.97	413.08	459.77	509.53	512.06	585.46	719.49
Low	325.92	396.52	444.38	489.17	502.43	573.38	674.64
Average	365.48	401.88	449.94	495.84	506.85	581.00	689.27

Figure 35: Annuity Payout Averages, 2012

The RBC Insurance website (www.rbcinsurance.com/annuities/payout-annuity-calculator.html) has a free annuity calculator that you can use without having to submit personal information and be contacted by a sales agent. We ran a sample calculation for a joint couple, both age 70, with $1 million in non-registered funds to invest. Specifying no guaranteed period of payout, the results were a lifetime monthly payment of $5,024.65, for an annual income of $61,803.57. This sum is not indexed for inflation, so the spending value will decrease every year.

The questions for us about when and if to buy an annuity went back, again, to how long we thought we would live, and up to what age we felt we could still handle managing our own finances. That will hopefully be a long way off, but our gut feel was that at some point, we would like to sit back, relax, and let someone else worry about our income flow.

Another option might be to keep our investments but hire a wealth management company to handle the details of making sure we have enough money to spend each month.

Wealth Management

Once we get too old to manage our own investments and cash flow anymore, we may consider hiring a wealth management company to do so for us. For an annual percentage of our portfolio, the wealth manager can take over the care of our investments and ensure that we are paid a monthly sum from it that will cover our expenses. The major banks as well as private wealth management companies offer this service.

Given our previous bad experience with financial advisors, we look to this option with a bit of concern. If we go this route, we will definitely do more research before making our selection of a company to help us. Current legislation in the works to implement more regulation and force greater transparency from financial advisors will hopefully help the situation in the future.

Retirement Homes

When researching retirement home options for our parents, we discovered that much has changed in this industry since the previous generation. Back in our parents' day, retirement homes used to be more like nursing homes in their institutional or hospital-like feel. It is no surprise that they now regard moving to one with wary reluctance.

These days retirement homes are more like holiday resorts for seniors, and we've visited everything from three-star to five-star establishments. As with anything, you get what you pay for, but the higher-end ones are quite luxurious. We visited one place that had a personal on-site chef who cooked all the meals from locally sourced food and made everything from scratch, including the breads, jams and butter. It had a fleet of Lincoln Town Cars to drive you around to your doctor's appointments or to go shopping. The activities offered included watercolour painting and cooking lessons, on-site lectures on interesting topics by experts in the field, and outings to theatres, museums and art galleries. We need to try to save some of our retirement money in our later years to get into one of these places!

For the most part, all the retirement homes that we visited provide the same basic health and personal care offerings. They all have 24/7 nursing care, a weekly on-site visit by a general practice doctor and all meals included, although some offer breakfast as an option in order to save on expenses. Most of them include weekly linen and towel service as well as light housekeeping. They all have common areas, including lounges, activity rooms, exercise rooms, movie theatres/chapels, libraries and outdoor patios.

The room sizes and monthly rental fee differ from place to place. The sizes seem to range from around 350 square feet up to 1000 square feet or more, with the average size being around 600 square feet. In 2012, the prices ranged from around $3500 up to $6500 with a $600–$750 supplement for a second occupant. The higher-end place described earlier even has some units with large balconies, but this is an anomaly and not usually available.

One of the considerations when picking a retirement home is the progression path as we age and potentially become sicker or otherwise more in need of care. Some homes are for only relatively healthy, mobile and self-sufficient residents. As soon as you don't qualify, you will be forced to move out, which could be traumatic when you are already ill. Others have special assisted-living floors, memory-care floors for dementia and Alzheimer's sufferers, or even full-fledged nursing home care. These allow for a smooth transition as your health declines while still keeping you within the same building and familiar surroundings.

Things may drastically change again by the time we are old enough to consider retirement homes, but this was useful information to learn about and to file away for the future. One final important point that we realized through our research for a suitable place for our parents is that you cannot wait until the last minute when you have to move due to health reasons. If you do, then the choices will be limited and you will be forced to go to any place that has availability. The nicer places may have long waiting lists, so it is wise to plan ahead. Also, what is the point of going to a retirement home that offers fun and exciting activities if you are too sick or frail to participate?

How Is It Going So Far?

It has been over half a year of retired bliss, and so far, everything is exactly as we planned and expected. Our lives are full, exciting and stress-free. We are actually busier than before we retired since we have more time and energy to plan adventures now. We never feel bored since there are so many activities to choose from. In fact, we have made only a dent in our list of new things that we would like to do or try.

We are definitely living a healthier lifestyle. We try to do some physical activity every day, eat less fast food and spend more time cooking wholesome, balanced meals. We're meeting one of our main goals for early retirement, which was to spend more quality time with our aging parents.

For the first time in 26 years, we are able to enjoy an entire summer off. We can take a trip for more than a week at a time and no longer have to worry about deadlines, deliverables, month ends, quotas or the workload that would be waiting for us when we returned to the office. We can decide to drive up north on a whim in the middle of the week, just because it is a nice day. We can enjoy being outside on a sunny "weekday" and not be depressed if it rains on our "weekend." We no longer experience the dreaded "Sunday evening blues" and are even starting to forget which day of the week it is.

We still haven't really learned how to slow down yet, and maybe we never will. We've always loved to be busy and active, although every once in a while it's nice to choose to stay at home all day, curled up with a book or watching a good movie. We still have the clock radio set to go off at the same time as when we were working, and wake up relatively early to start off the day. But one of our favourite moments is lying in bed listening to the traffic report about the latest morning snarl-up, and then rolling over and falling back to sleep for another half hour.

From a financial perspective, it's early days yet, but so far, so good. We are continuing to execute the same dividend strategy that has worked for us through our savings years. The only difference now is that instead of reinvesting our dividends to save more, we withdraw them to spend on our expenses. Although the markets are still depressed and continue to swing wildly in reaction to the latest global crisis, our dividends hold firm and pay out on schedule like clockwork. For the most part, our expenses remain within range of our estimates. We have budgeted enough so that we can have an enjoyable lifestyle without feeling the need to skimp, although we need to think twice before we unexpectedly splurge.

It has always been our wish to retire early, while we are still healthy and active enough to enjoy it. It took much effort and perseverance to get here — some might say too much effort, and who has the time? But we always had our eye on the finish line, and now that we are here, we can say without a doubt that it was all worth it.

References

We began our research by reviewing the following sources:

Title	Authors/Description
Books	
Dividend Stocks For Dummies (Wiley, 2010)	Lawrence Carrel
Money Management For Canadians All-in-One Desk Reference For Dummies, 1st Edition (Wiley, 2003)	Andrew Bell, Andrew Dagys, Tony Ioannou with Moira Bayne, Wendy Yano, Margaret Kerr, JoAnn Kurtz, John Lawrence Reynolds
The Motley Fool's Money After 40: Building Wealth for a Better Life (Simon & Schuster, 2006)	David Gardner
The New Pension Strategy for Canadians (Insomniac, 2009)	Andrew Springett
New Rules for Retirement: What Your Financial Advisor Isn't Telling You (Collins, 2008)	Warren Mackenzie, Ken Hawkins
The Retirement Time Bomb : Achieving Financial Independence in a Changing World (Penguin, 2006)	Gordon Pape
The 7 Most Important Equations for Your Retirement: The Fascinating People and Ideas Behind Planning Your Retirement Income (Wiley, 2012)	Moshe A. Milevsky
Sleep-Easy Investing: Your Stress-Free Guide to Financial Success (Viking Canada, 2008)	Gordon Pape

Smart Women Finish Rich: 9 Steps to Achieving Financial Security and Funding Your Dreams (Doubleday Canada, 2003)	David Bach
The Wealthy Barber: The Common Sense Guide to Successful Financial Planning, Special Gold Edition (Stoddart, 1998)	David Chilton

Magazines and Newspapers	
Globe and Mail newspaper	Business section
MoneySense magazine	Retirement tips; stock picks (top 200 dividend stocks, etc.), investment articles
TV Network	
Business News Network	Investment news, advice and call-in shows

We found the following websites useful in our research:

Website	URL	Description
Investment Sites – information about stocks, bonds, investments		
Canadian Dividend Reinvestment Plans	cdndrips.blogspot.ca	Information about DRIPs and listing of stocks that provide DRIPs
Cannex Financial Exchanges	www.cannex.com	Free deposit account interest rates
Globe and Mail Investor	www.theglobeandmail.com/globe-investor	Stock info, watchlists, investment tools and news
Globe and	www.theglobeandmail.com/globe-	Create a

Website	URL	Description
Mail Watchlist	investor/my-watchlist	personal portfolio of your stocks so that you can monitor their performance
Morningstar	www.morningstar.ca	Stock info, news
StockChase	www.stockchase.com	Analyst comments about stocks
Retirement Sites		
Annuities – RBC Insurance	http://www.rbcinsurance.com/annuities/payout-annuity-calculator.html	Annuity calculator to predict premiums or payouts
Globe Investor Retirement Calculator	www.globeinvestor.com/resources/personalfinance/rrsp/retirement_calc/CARetirementPlan.html	Based on input parameters, generates report of retirement income base and how long the money will last
Life Expectancy Calculator	www.livingto100.com	Detailed questions about lifestyle, medical history, family
Life Expectancy Calculator	media.nmfn.com/tnetwork/lifespan	Short, quick survey

Website	URL	Description
Retirement Blog	retirehappyblog.ca	Helpful tips and information about retirement
RRIF Calculator	www.moneyville.ca/financialcalculators/retirement/858691	Quick calculation of RRIF minimum payments
Tax Calculator – LSM Insurance	lsminsurance.ca/calculators/canada/income-tax	Determine how much gross income you need in order to generate net revenue for spending
Tax Calculator – Walter Harder & Associates	www.walterharder.ca/T1.asp	Does a rough estimate of taxes; the current year is fee-based, but the previous years are free
TaxTips.ca	www.taxtips.ca	Canadian tax and financial information; see www.taxtips.ca/taxrates/on.htm for marginal tax rates for Ontario

Government Websites		
Financial Services Commission of Ontario – Pensions	www.fsco.gov.on.ca/en/pensions/Pages/Default.aspx	Regulatory board of Ontario Ministry of Finance; info on LIRAs and LIFs
My Service Canada Account Login	www.servicecanada.gc.ca/eng/online/mysca.shtml	Log in to view your personal account re: CPP, OAS, etc.
Revenue Canada – My Account	www.cra-arc.gc.ca/myaccount	View past tax statements
Home Swap and Travel Sites		
Expedia	www.expedia.ca	Discount flights, car rentals, hotels
Geenee	www.geenee.com	Free home swap website
Home Exchange	www.homeexchange.com	Fee-based home swap website
HomeForExchange.com	www.homeforexchange.com	Fee-based home swap website
Hotels.com	www.hotels.com	Discount hotels
Intervac	www.intervac-homeexchange.com	Fee-based home swap website
Love Home Swap	www.lovehomeswap.com	Fee-based home swap website
Priceline	www.priceline.com	Discount flights, car rentals, hotels

Vacation Rentals by Owner	www.vrbo.com	Vacation rental properties offered directly by the owner, often resulting in lower prices than hotels since there is no intermediary agency to pay Nicer than staying in a hotel since you get an entire apartment or house including kitchen and living room

Iguana Books

iguanabooks.com

If you enjoyed *Retired at 48: One Couple's Journey to a Pensionless Retirement ...*

Look for other books coming soon from Iguana Books! Subscribe to our blog for updates as they happen.

iguanabooks.com/blog/

You can also learn more about A.R. English and her upcoming work on her blog.

arenglish.iguanabooks.com/blog/

If you're a writer ...

Iguana Books is always looking for great new writers, in every genre. We produce primarily ebooks but, as you can see, we do the occasional print book as well. Visit us at iguanabooks.com to see what Iguana Books has to offer both emerging and established authors.

iguanabooks.com/publishing-with-iguana/

If you're looking for another good book ...

All Iguana Books books are available on our website. We pride ourselves on making sure that every Iguana book is a great read.

iguanabooks.com/bookstore/

Visit our bookstore today and support your favourite author.

IGUANA

www.ingramcontent.com/pod-product-compliance
Lightning Source LLC
Chambersburg PA
CBHW072045040426
42447CB00012BB/3020

* 9 7 8 1 9 2 7 4 0 3 4 5 7 *